S0-ADN-554

Austen
COUNTRY

Austen
COUNTRY
Tom Howard

Grange BOOKS

AUSTEN (UK)

PHOTOGRAPHIC ACKNOWLEDGEMENTS
Jacket front cover main picture: Derek Forss Photography
Jacket front cover black and white inset:
Hulton Deutsch Collection
Back cover: Derek Forss Photography

Inside pages
Bridgeman Art Library
40 bottom, 52

Comstock Photo Library
26-27, 28, 38 bottom, 40 top, 47

John Crook
77 both, 80

Edifice
10, 11, 12, 13, 15, 16, 17, 18 both, 19, 21, 22-23, 24, 29, 43, 48 bottom, 49, 62 both, 64, 65 (Sarah Jackson), 46 both, 48 both top, 73 bottom, 75 (Philippa Lewis)

Derek Forss Photography
4-5, 35, 44 top, 55, 56, 57, 73 top

Jarrolds Publishing
36, 37, 38 top, 44 bottom, 58, 59, 60, 61

A.F. Kersting
2-3, 25, 30, 31, 32, 33, 34, 42-43, 45, 51, 53, 54, 66, 69, 74, 78, 79

National Building's Record
72

Clare Pawley
70 both, 71

Malcom Porter
Map on pages 8-9

Sarah Jackson would like to thank: Penelope Hughs Hallett; Mrs Joyce Brown, The Jane Austen Society, Steventon; Mr Tom Carpenter, Jane Austen Memorial Trust; Mr & Mrs Robert French-Blake, Ibthorpe House, Ibthorpe, Hampshire; Mr & Mrs Christopher Scott, Ashe Park

**Pages 2-3: View from Box Hill.
These pages: The Royal Crescent, Bath, Avon.**

Published in 1997
by Grange Books
An imprint of Grange Books Plc.
The Grange
Grange Yard
London SE1 3AG

ISBN 1 85627 783 6

Text copyright © 1995, 1997 Tom Howard
The right of Tom Howard of be identified as the author of this work has been asserted by him in accordance with the Copyright, Design and Patents Act, 1988

Copyright © 1995, 1997 Regency House Publishing Limited

All rights reserved. No part of this publication may be reproduced, stored in a retrieval system, or transmitted in any form or by any means, electronic, mechanical, photocopying, recording or otherwise, without the prior permission of the copyright holder.

Printed in China

CONTENTS

INTRODUCTION

OPPOSITE

A portrait of Jane Austen by Cassandra Austen, sketched in 1810. Although used as the main source for the prettified portrait accompanying James Edward Austen-Leigh's 1870 *A Memoir of Jane Austen*, and presumably regarded by the family as acceptable, it may not be a particularly good likeness, though one can well imagine this to be a person of sharp wit and perception. James Edward describes her as *'very attractive; her figure was rather tall and slender ... a clear brunette with a rich colour; she had full round cheeks, with mouth and nose small and well-formed, bright, hazel eyes, and brown hair forming natural curls round her face'.*

J ane Austen's novels were not great romantic sagas or picaresque adventures. Neither were they examinations of the great moral issues of her time. They were minutely-observed portraits of middle-class English provincial life. She was wise enough to write about what she knew best, and portrayed each of her characters with incomparable wit, delicacy and wry humour.

That her work is so highly regarded and attracts such enthusiastic readership to this day can be attributed to the quality of her writing. To read her novels is to vividly imagine oneself the confidant of each of her characters, eagerly absorbing all the neighbourhood gossip from an endlessly fascinating raconteur. So close is the narrator's voice that it seems perfectly natural when, in the middle of *Sense and Sensibility*, for just one sentence, she adopts the personal pronoun.

The most successful novelist of his day, Sir Walter Scott, was enviously to declare:

'That young lady had a talent for describing the involvements, and feelings, and characters of ordinary life, which to me is the most wonderful I ever met with. The Big Bow-wow strain I can do myself like any now going: but the exquisite touch, which renders ordinary commonplace things and characters so interesting, from the truth of the description and the sentiment, is denied to me.'

Anthony Trollope and Alfred, Lord Tennyson were other literary admirers, and E.M. Forster, whose early 20th century novels were deeply concerned with the middle-class psyche, declared: *'She is my favourite author! I read and re-read, the mouth open and the mind closed. Shut up in measureless content, I greet her by the name of most kind hostess, while criticism slumbers.'*

She did have her detractors. Elizabeth Barrett Browning and Charlotte Brontë for instance, considered her to be of limited talent and, though her novels were generally well received on publication (the Prince Regent is said to have kept a complete set in each of his several residences), it was not until many years after her death and the publication of her nephew's biography of her life that she began to attract a following and the reputation of a classic writer that goes with her name today.

Jane Austen lived through very dramatic times: the French Revolution and the American fight for independence were taking place when she was a child, followed by the Napoleonic Wars in which her brothers saw service as sailors with the British Navy. In India, Britain was beginning to establish her Imperial power. At home, the enclosure of common land by the propertied gentry was changing the countryside and worsening the lot of the labouring countryman while steam-power, canals and industrialization were changing the economic pattern still further. Though by background a high Tory, she makes frequent criticism of blatant self-interest and exploitation, but her concern is with relationships and behaviour on a personal level, rather than with wider events and politics. These things play little part in her writing, but they are part of the background to them, as they were part of the background of her contemporary readers. To quote Sir Walter Scott again:

'The subjects are not often elegant, and certainly never grand; but they are finished up to nature, and with a precision which delights the reader.'

That precision is concentrated on conversation and behaviour. Jane Austen wastes few words describing the workings of the outside world, except where they have some bearing on the personality or station of her characters. There are no detailed text pictures of architecture or landscape which can pinpoint the precise identity of the locations she may have had in mind when writing about them.

Many of the scenes of Jane Austen's novels are set in well-known places: London, Bath, Portsmouth, Lyme Regis, but the country houses and small villages are given fictional names. However, she clearly wrote from her own experience, drawing closely on places that she knew, though she often combines elements of several actual locations to produce a setting for her story. In *Mansfield Park* she placed the scene of the action in Northamptonshire, a county she did not know, and while writing the novel requested in a letter to her sister: 'If you could discover whether Northamptonshire is a country of Hedgerows I should be glad'. However, she was able to draw upon knowledge of the country mansion her brother had inherited from adoptive parents and many other grand houses to create Sir Thomas Bertram's residence: but it is more usual for her to use familiar locales.

You will not find pictures of Northamptonshire in the pages that follow but, as this book explores her life, her

homes and travels, you will find many photographs of places familiar to Jane Austen as they exist today. Two centuries have wrought great changes but it is still possible to view them as a background to her life and a further dimension to her work.

Austen COUNTRY

Pulteney Bridge, Bath

Stoneleigh

Kenilworth

Warwick

Adelstrop

Oxf

R. Thames

The Cobb, Lyme Regis

Bristol

Bath

R. Avon

Andover

Whitchu

Salisbury

Winches

Southampton

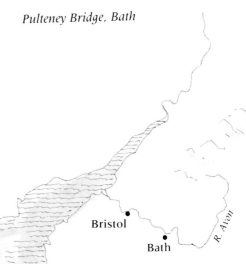

Exeter

Northleigh

Sidmouth

Lyme Regis

Bournemouth

Dawlish

Teignmouth

N

BATH

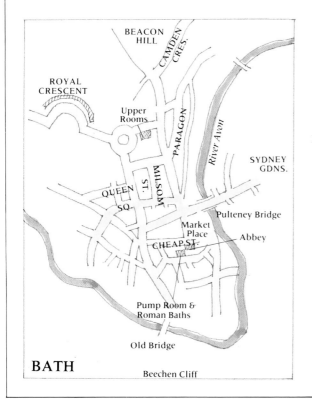

BEACON HILL

CAMDEN CRES.

ROYAL CRESCENT

Upper Rooms

PARAGON

River Avon

SYDNEY GDNS.

MILSOM ST.

QUEEN SQ.

Pulteney Bridge

Market Place

Abbey

CHEAP ST.

Pump Room & Roman Baths

Old Bridge

Beechen Cliff

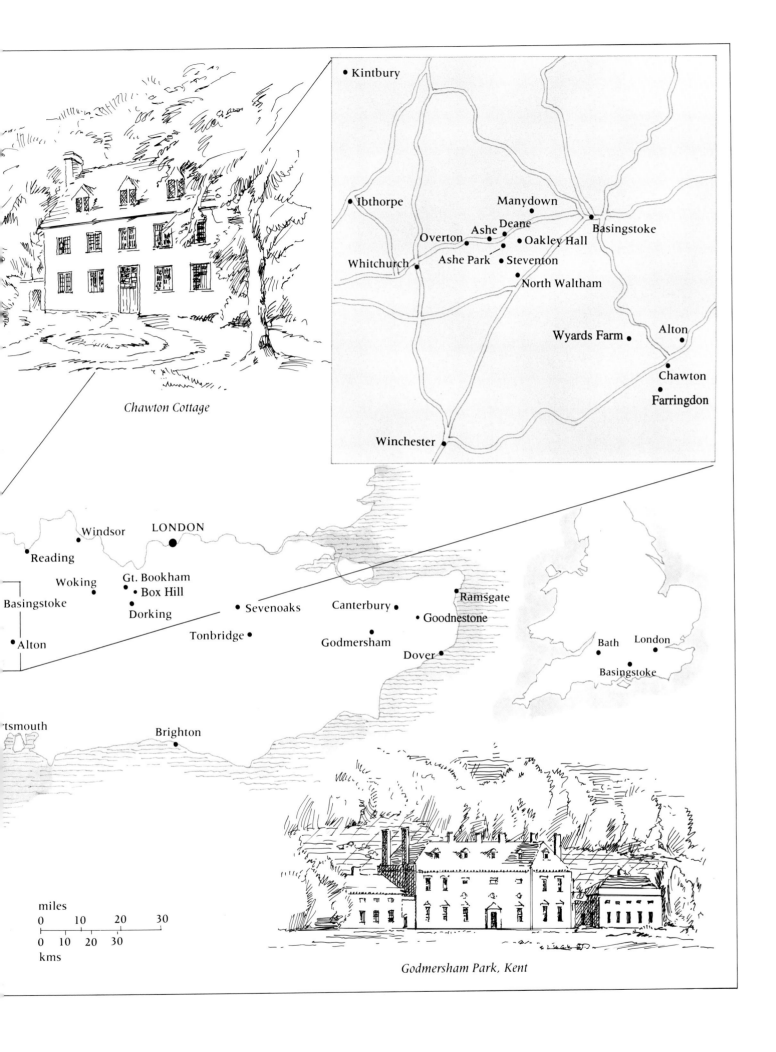

Chawton Cottage

Kintbury

Ibthorpe
Manydown
Ashe Deane
Overton Ashe Basingstoke
Oakley Hall
Whitchurch Ashe Park Steventon
North Waltham

Wyards Farm Alton

Chawton

Farringdon

Winchester

Windsor LONDON

Reading

Woking Gt. Bookham
Box Hill
Basingstoke
Dorking Sevenoaks Canterbury Ramsgate
Goodnestone
Alton Tonbridge Godmersham Bath London
Dover
Basingstoke

rtsmouth Brighton

miles
0   10   20   30

0   10   20   30
kms

Godmersham Park, Kent

STEVENTON

A pump in a field at Steventon. A metal replacement of an earlier wooden pump is all that remains of the rectory where Jane Austen was born, the house being demolished in the 19th century not very long after her death.

Jane Austen was born in the rectory of Steventon, a village in the English county of Hampshire on 16 December 1775. Her father, George Austen, was descended from a family who had been clothing manufacturers in Kent, in the south-east of the country, in the middle ages. Some of its members had become wealthy landowners but he came from a less prosperous branch, some of whom had entered the professions. His father was a surgeon, an occupation of little social status at that time, and an uncle was a solicitor. George was orphaned when he was six years old and his uncle sent him to school at Tonbridge and then on to St. John's College, Oxford, where he obtained a scholarship. After a period spent teaching at his old school, he returned to Oxford and took Holy Orders. Clergymen were not then paid by the central church authority but received an income from the rents, tithes and any other profits accruing to the benefice which had usually been given by the founder who established the church or were the gift of other benefactors. This gave the founder's inheritors, whether by descent or purchase, the right to choose the incumbent; one of George Austen's richer relatives, his uncle, Francis, owned the gift of the living at Steventon and in 1761 he presented it to him. His uncle also bought him two other livings in the neighbouring parishes of Ashe and Deane to add further to his income, once the present incumbents had died.

Jane's mother, Cassandra Leigh,

whom George married in Bath in 1764, came from a family which could trace its roots back to the Norman conquest. One ancestor had been Lord Mayor of London in the time of Elizabeth I, and a great-aunt had married the Duke of Chandos. His wife's branch of the family was settled at Adelstrop in Gloucestershire while a junior branch had their country seat at Stoneleigh Abbey in Warwickshire. Cassandra was brought up at Harpsden in the Thames Valley not far from Windsor, where her father was rector, holding the living of All Soul's College, Oxford where he had been a Fellow. She may have met her husband at Oxford where her uncle Theophilus, was Master of Balliol. A decade earlier, her brother James had inherited an estate at Northleigh, Oxfordshire, from another relation, adopting their surname of Perrot as a condition of his inheritance.

By comparison with some members of their families, Jane's parents were 'poor relations', but they were by no means impoverished, having had good education and important 'connections'. Her father's annual income was between £500 and £600 but he added to this by taking boys of good family as paying pupils to be tutored and live as members of his household. The first of them was probably the son of Warren Hastings, the British administrator in India, though there is no surviving proof of this, and others included the son of Lord Portsmouth whose country seat was within a few miles at Hurstbourne Park. With the help of a paid foreman he also ran the rectory lands as a farm thus providing some further income as well as helping to feed the family and servants.

There were already five elder brothers and a sister when Jane was born in 1775: James (born 1765), George (1766), Edward (1768), Henry (1771), Francis (1774), Cassandra (1775), and Charles was to follow four years later. Little is known about George, apart from a reference in a letter of 1770 in which Mrs. Austen mentions that he was prone to fits. Was he handicapped in some way, and perhaps deaf? Many years later Jane writes of being able to speak to the deaf with her fingers. He lived until 1838, but maybe not as part of the household. Edward became a landed gentleman, adopted by his wealthy uncle and taking his surname of Knight; two brothers went into the church and two into the Navy; Cassandra did not marry but stayed at home. The lives of this large family could not have failed to interact with Jane's, widening her knowledge of the world and extending her range of acquaintances.

The England of 1775 was still ruled by George II. The Boston Tea Party which sparked the fight for American Independence had taken place only two years earlier and the slave trade still flourished from English ports. Though steam power had been used to pump water out of mines since the beginning of the century, James Watt's improvements to the steam engine, which were to make it the driving force of the next century, and Richard Arkwright's patent for his water frame both date from 1769. The building of the first iron bridge was to come ten years later. But the technical changes brought about by the Industrial Revolution, which took place during her lifetime, were more noticeable in the North and Midlands

than in the area frequented by Jane Austen. In her milieu, social status was firmly based on property rather than commerce. However, a comparable revolution was taking place on the land of which she, and therefore her characters, would have been well aware. The old medieval system of common land and the farming of strips in larger shared fields was already being swept away in the reign of Elizabeth I. But by the last quarter of the 18th century many successive Acts of Parliament were forcing the enclosure of the land by purchase or exchange of territory as decreed by Parliamentary Commissioners to enable the big landowners to make the transition to new agricultural methods.

The approach to Steventon Church, where Jane Austen's father was rector for 40 years.

The site of Steventon rectory. The house was near the road, approached by a 'sweep', a curving drive big enough to accommodate carriages, from a gate in an wooden fence of open palings. A trellis arch framed the front door, which led straight into the parlour. Jane and Cassandra shared a bedroom and a sitting-room on the first floor, where they had bookshelves and space for Jane's piano and writing desk. The Reverend Austen had a book-lined study overlooking the garden at the back of the house, where two wings extended to the rear.

There were 1,300 Enclosure Acts between 1760 and 1801, when the General Enclosure Act simplified the procedures involved, and a further 1,000 in the next two decades. As a contemporary verse put it:

They hang the man and flog the woman
That steals a goose from off the common
But leave the greater criminal loose
That steals the common from the goose.

Enclosure meant that land could become the property of the individual, thus changing the face of society to this day. It changed the landscape too, for as fields were enclosed, woodlands and wastes disappeared and a new pattern of hedges, walls, fences and roads took shape. Together with the fashionable new landscaping of parkland in the style of Capability Brown, emulating the idealized landscapes of Claude and Poussin, this created what many think of as the natural appearance of the English countryside: a prospect which itself saw rapid change two centuries later with the grubbing up of hedgerows to create the larger fields required by highly mechanized farming methods.

Agricultural techniques apart, the growth of arable crops as winter feed for cattle brought fresh instead of salt meat for winter meals and a reduction of scurvy and other skin diseases – though a preference for more highly refined flour, instead of wholemeal, was to prove bad for health and teeth. Not that the increasing number of landless labourers could afford such luxuries.

The establishment of passenger services on steam-hauled railways did not begin until a decade after Jane Austen's death, but canals and improved river navigation were already having their effect and bringing great improvement to both roads and road transportation services. This made it much easier to travel about the country, especially on the new turnpike roads that were being built in such numbers at the time and for which travellers were expected to pay a toll. Travel over long distances was not a thing to be taken lightly, especially by ladies of refinement, but visits to London, to fashionable watering places, or to stay with friends in their country houses were becoming more a question of expense than availability of transport. The Austens lived in a small village but they were by no means cut off from the world. News travelled quickly along the highways, whether of foreign wars or private gossip.

As babies, all the Austen children were put out to a wet-nurse who lived a mile away in Deane. This was a common practice among gentlefolk at this time and, although not under the same roof, they were not cut off entirely from their parents, for one or other made a daily visit to see them. Once weaned, the babies would have been returned to the rectory.

While she was still a very little child, two of Jane's brothers, James and Edward, both left home. James, aged 14, went up to Oxford to become a

Founder's Kin scholar (through his mother's family connections) at his father's old college, St. John's. Edward went to live with the Knight family (whose heir he later became) at Godmersham Park in Kent. George too, may not have been brought up at home. Though Frank was nearer to Jane in years she seems to have been closest to Henry and Cassandra. Henry was her favourite brother and Cassandra her immediate role model. 'If Cassandra were going to have her head cut off, Jane would insist on sharing her fate', was the way Mrs. Austen put it. So much so, that when Cassandra was sent away to school in 1782, six-year-old Jane went too. The school was run by Mrs. Cawley, the widow of an academic and sister of their mother's brother-in-law, Edward Cooper. They were soon

The ground behind the rectory rises and the terrace which formed the Austens' 'Wood Walk' can still be discerned. This was set out as a shrubbery with occasional seats or benches. In *Northanger Abbey* Catherine Morland enjoys rolling down just such a green slope as that which descended to the house.

joined there by their cousin Jane Cooper.

The following year Mrs. Cawley relocated her school to Southampton, and it was there that an epidemic of a condition called 'putrid throat', a septic throat characteristic of typhus fever, broke out. This was a common infection which the Austens had unhappily already experienced – it had killed Warren Hastings's little boy, aged six, when he was in their charge. Jane Cooper informed her mother in a letter and Mrs. Cooper and Mrs. Austen collected their daughters and took them home as soon as possible. The girls survived but Mrs. Cooper herself caught the infection and died of it.

The girls did not return to Southampton. Another school was found: the Abbey School in Reading, located in the gatehouse of Reading Abbey. From an account left by a pupil who attended this school a little after Jane Austen, it was an easy-going establishment where, provided pupils appeared at mealtimes and put in an hour or two's study with their tutor in the morning, they were free to spend the rest of the day as they wished. Certainly, when Jane's brother Edward called to see them together with Jane Cooper's brother and a party of friends, the girls were given leave to join them in a meal at a local inn.

Jane continued at the Abbey until she was 11 and was then taught at home by her father. She learned French, a little Italian, read the classics – and contemporary fiction. Her mother probably supervised her sewing and embroidery (at which she became most proficient) and other feminine accomplishments. She also learned to play the piano and as she grew older took great pleasure in dancing.

The vicar's family took an active part in local life. The boys were keen sportsmen. When he was seven years old, Francis had bought himself a pony on which he regularly went hunting and little Charles was soon infected with the same enthusiasm. However, by the time Jane was living at home, Francis was already at the Royal Naval College, Portsmouth, where Charles followed him in 1791, though of course they did come home on leave from time to time.

The Austens were on receiving terms with families in the locality who were rather more prosperous than themselves and, as the girls grew up, they received many invitations to attend both private and public balls. They also mounted theatrical performances at home in the barn behind the house at midsummer and in the dining-room in winter. These seem to have begun in 1784 with a performance of Richard Brinsley Sheridan's *The Rivals* and to have sporadically continued until 1790. (Later, Jane's memories of them provided her with useful material for some of the scenes in *Mansfield Park*).

Her brother James wrote prologues for some of these performances and Jane appears to have assisted with them. Composing rhymed charades was also a family pastime to which Jane contributed. At 12 years old she was the busy author of stories and amusing sketches, frequently dedicated to friends or family members, which sometimes parodied popular contemporary novels. However, they were not particularly well-regarded. In a family such as hers, such talents and pursuits were not considered exceptional. Up at Oxford her brother James founded and edited a journal: *The Loiterer*. Henry later wrote for it and he and Charles were both versifiers. Cassandra, according to Jane herself was 'the finest comic writer of the age' (though nothing survives to prove it!). Later a niece began to send

The lane which led from the rectory to Steventon church was not much more than a rutted track when the Austens lived here. In bad weather they would wear pattens to keep their feet out of the mud – clog-like overshoes with iron rings beneath to walk on and raise the sole out of the dirt. In dry weather they would use a path straight from their garden to the church.

her own stories, seeking her opinion of them, and a nephew wrote the first biography of his Aunt Jane. By 1793 she had copied some of these early writings into notebooks which still survive, entitled *Volume the First, Volume the Second* and *Volume the Third*. A comic *History of England, Love and Friendship*, a novel in letter form parodying popular romances, and the rather more ambitious but incomplete *Catherine* are all among these early pieces.

In 1791, Jane's brother Edward, having been sent on the Grand Tour to Europe rather than to university, married Elizabeth Bridges, daughter of a wealthy landowner of Goodnestone, Kent and they set up home at Rowlings quite close to her own family and his adoptive parents at Godmersham. James, after a time as Fellow of his old Oxford college, became a clergyman and, in 1792, moved back nearer to Steventon as curate to the parish of Overton. That same year he married, his wife Eliza bringing £100 a year to add to his own income of £200, and they moved into the rectory which went with the living at Deane which had been bought for his father. This had been occupied by the widow of Rev. Nowys Lloyd and her daughters, but they now moved to Ibthorpe, some miles to the west enabling him to take up residence.

The Lloyds were close friends of the Austens, as too were the family of the

Ashe House, home of the Reverend Isaac Lefroy and his family. Mrs. Lefroy became Jane's close friend: her death following a fall from her horse in 1804 came as a great shock. This was where she met Tom Lefroy (see pages 18-19). The youngest of the Lefroy boys married Jane's niece Anna. Usually the double doors between the dining- and morning-rooms were opened to allow plenty of room for dancing, but a letter of 1800 describes a lively party of 14 taking place in the study, the dining-room being out of action because a storm had blown down the chimney. It had also played havoc with the elms at Steventon rectory. Ashe House ceased to be the local rectory in 1905.

Rev. George Lefroy who held the adjoining living in the parish of Ashe. Among the local gentry the Austens were also well acquainted with the Bigg-Withers of Manydown Park, the Bramstones of Oakley Hall, the Harwoods of Deane House, the Holders of Ashe Park, the Portals of Freefolk, and on an even grander level with Lord Bolton of Hackwood, Lady Dorchester of Greywell (later of Kempshott) and the Portsmouths, to whose son Mr. Austen had been a tutor.

A guest at Steventon in 1792 was Jane Cooper, who stayed there between the time of her father's death in August and her marriage in December. Another was Eliza de Feuillide, daughter of the Rev. Austen's sister,

Philadelphia. Her father, now deceased, had met and married her mother in India, where they met Warren Hastings and his wife who proved themselves to be generous friends. They had often stayed at Steventon before Eliza was sent to Paris to complete her education and where she met her husband, a French aristocrat, the Comte de Feuillide. She returned to England when she was expecting a baby and, especially after her mother's death in 1791 she, with her son, were often at Steventon again.

In France, the Revolution was building up to the execution of Louis XVI at the beginning of 1793. The Comte returning to France in an attempt to sort out his own affairs and

Ashe Park, home of local friends the Holders, is a large, red-brick mansion dating back to the reign of James I. 'To sit in idleness over a good fire in a well-proportioned room is a luxurious sensation,' Jane Austen wrote after a November evening spent there in 1800.

salvage what he could of his estates, foolishly supported the Marquis de Marboeuf who had been charged with failing to cooperate with the State over food production. He became further embroiled in the affair and was guillotined early in 1794. The political upheavals in France may not have troubled the consciences of the landed British aristocracy but they were certainly well informed of the French situation and were keeping a close watch for signs of creeping egalitarism in their own country. The execution of such a close relation must have brought the reality of the Terror dramatically to the consciousness of the family in their country vicarage.

The following year brought another family tragedy: the death of James's wife Anne. His little daughter, two-year-old Jane Anna Elizabeth, was taken across from Deane to Steventon to be brought up by her grandparents and aunts. Happier news arrived of the acquittal of Eliza's family's benefactor, Warren Hastings, impeached by the British Parliament in 1788 for alleged corruption in his administration of India and now released after a trial lasting seven years.

There were also developments in the Austen sisters' own private lives. Cassandra was becoming attached to a young clergyman, Thomas Fowle, the brother of Mrs. Lloyd's son-in-law. In

RIGHT
Though the coaching inn where the Austens used to collect their mail now stands near a busy motorway, most of the local roads still pass through peaceful countryside.

BELOW
The Winterborne Valley near Ibthorpe to which the Lloyd family moved after leaving the rectory at Deane.

fact she had known Tom since childhood; he had been a pupil of her father's at Steventon before she went away to school. They became engaged in 1795 but Jane began a flirtation with another Tom, an Irish cousin of the Lefroy family at Ashe Rectory.

It is not clear how serious Jane's involvement with the handsome young Irishman was. Letters surviving from the time reveal that Jane wrote regularly to Cassandra when they were apart; but her references to Lefroy are extremely flippant and light-hearted. Both Cassandra and Mrs. Lefroy were concerned and gently warned her against involvement for both were lacking in financial resources even though Tom Lefroy was clearly over-ambitious. This rather suggests that she ran a serious risk of disappointment,

Ibthorpe House, the new home
of Martha Lloyd, her mother and
sisters which Jane was often
to visit.

but her outward defence of the liaison bears all the hallmarks of a person nursing a real but self-acknowledged 'impossible' affection.

In the first of her letters to survive, dated 9 January 1796, Jane replied to her sister, who was staying with her fiancé's family at Kintbury in Berkshire:

'You scold me so much ... that I am almost afraid to tell you how my Irish friend and I behaved. Imagine to yourself everything most profligate and shocking in the way of dancing and sitting down together. I can expose myself, however, only once more, because he leaves the country soon after next Friday, on which day we are to dance at Ashe after all. He is a very gentleman-like, good-looking, pleasant young man, I assure you. But as to our having ever met, except at the three last balls, I cannot say much; for he is so excessively laughed at about me at Ashe, that he is ashamed of

coming to Steventon, and ran away when we called on Mrs. Lefroy a few days ago ...

' ... he has but one *fault, which time will, I trust, entirely remove – it is that his morning coat is a great deal too light. He is a very great admirer of Tom Jones* [the title character in the novel by Henry Fielding], *and therefore wears the same coloured clothes, I imagine, which he did when he was wounded ...'*

A week later she writes:

'Tell Mary that I make over Mr. Heartley ... to her ... and ... all my other admirers ... as I mean to confine myself in future to Mr. Tom Lefroy, for whom I do not care sixpence ...

'At length the day is come on which I am to flirt my last with Tom Lefroy, and when you receive this it will be over. My tears flow as I write at the melancholy idea.'

Serious or not – and the Lefroy family later tended to believe that

Thomas *had* behaved rather badly as far as she was concerned – there had definitely been a strong attraction there. A nephew, who questioned Lefroy in old age reported that 'he did not state in what her fascination consisted, but he said in so many words that he was in love with her, although he qualified his confession by saying that it was a boyish love.' Whether or not hearts were broken, there was to be no future for this relationship. Tom Lefroy eventually made a suitable marriage and went on to pursue a legal career, eventually becoming Lord Chief Justice of Ireland.

Neither was Cassandra's happiness to last. Tom Fowles already had a living in Wiltshire and despite the promise from Lord Craven of a better one in the future, in Shropshire, it was not felt that his income could not yet support them. With some reluctance he accepted an invitation from Craven to go out to the West Indies as chaplain of his regiment in the hope that this would enable the couple to save money for their marriage.

He sailed in 1796 to commence his duties but on arriving at his destination went down with yellow fever and in 1797 died in Santo Domingo, the old island of Hispaniola which is now split between Haiti and the Dominican Republic. Cassandra was no doubt distraught when the news arrived. But as Jane related to Eliza Fowle (married to Tom's brother), Cassandra 'behaves with a degree of resolution and propriety, which no common mind could evince in so trying a situation.' It cannot have been much of a consolation that Craven regretted that he had sent a betrothed man abroad, neither was the £1,000 bequeathed to her by Tom – though in later years the income from it became a useful addition to the family finances. Cassandra never married and there is no report of her even considering the possibility of matrimony again.

However, there *were* Austen marriages that year. James was married to Mary Lloyd and Henry to his cousin Eliza, the Comtesse de Feuillide. Not that either wife was a first choice. James had first asked Eliza to become his second wife – but she refused him, not being particularly eager to become a parson's wife. Henry had been engaged in a flirtation with another woman, but perhaps without serious intentions, before he became engaged to Eliza, who was ten years his senior.

Jane persevered with her writing. It is not easy to assign accurate dates to particular works for she often made later amendments to her earlier writings. *Catherine*, which was written for the most part when she was 16, contains a reference to a book not published until 1809. Between 1794 and 1796 she completed *Elinor and Marianne*, a novel written as a sequence of letters which was complete enough to be read aloud to the family. (This story was later to be re-worked as *Sense and Sensibility*.) Another novel in letter form, *Lady Susan,* survives only in a clean copy written on paper bearing a watermark dating it to 1805. It was, in fact, written earlier, probably before Elinor and Marianne.

In the autumn of 1796, Jane began a new novel which she called *First Impressions* (later to become *Pride and Prejudice*). It was finished by the following August and her father thought so highly of it that he made an attempt to get it published, describing it as a three-volume novel of about the length of Fanny Burney's *Evelina*. The publisher promptly rejected the offer to read the manuscript. Jane's letters show that her intimates did not share the publisher's lack of interest but were eager to read and re-read it over the following years.

Jokingly she accused Martha Lloyd of being 'very cunning, but I saw through her design; she means to publish it from memory, and one more perusal must enable her to do it.'

While close members of the family were aware of all this literary activity, they did not wish the world at large to know. James's little daughter Anna, who became a great favourite of her Aunt Jane, heard Cassandra laughing as Jane read out parts of her work to her and soon became familiar with the story and its characters; but she was forbidden to divulge the secret. Anna herself began to compose stories, dictating them to her aunt: a copy still survives of a play written out for her by Jane.

In November 1797, Mrs. Austen took Jane and Cassandra on a visit to Bath, where it is likely that they stayed with Mrs. Austen's brother James Leigh Perrot and his wife. James had

Oakley Church, from the grounds of Oakley Hall.

Oakley Hall, now housing Hilsea College, was home to the Bramstons, another house which Jane knew well as a visitor. Here, she wrote to her sister in 1800, *'We did a great deal – ate some sandwiches all over mustard, admired Mr. Bramston's transparencies, and gained a promise ... of two roots of heartsease, one all yellow and the other all purple ...'*

adopted the surname Perrot on inheriting his great-uncle Perrot's estate in Oxfordshire. Although their main home was at Scarlets, in Berkshire, the Leigh Perrots spent half the year at Paragon Buildings in Bath. They too, were childless, and it was expected that they would make James Austen their heir. This may have been Jane's first visit to the city; if so, it was to be the first of many.

About this time Jane seems to have returned to *Elinor and Marianne* changing it from its letter form and incorporating her experiences of Bath: however, it was still many years from publication. We do not know its exact form when she felt it to be complete or put it aside to begin work on another story *Susan* (no connection to the earlier *Lady Susan*.) This was somewhat different from her other books in that it was a deliberate burlesque of the 'gothick' novel, no doubt influenced by the publication of Mrs. Radcliffe's *The Mysteries of Udolpho* in 1794. It was probably largely completed in 1799, and although in her introduction of 1816 Jane says it was 'finished' in 1805, it seems to have had much less revision than the other redrafted novels.

At the end of August 1798, Jane and Cassandra went with their parents to visit their brother Edward at Godmersham, the house and estate in Kent of which he had become the owner when his adoptive mother, Mrs. Knight, moved to White Friars in Canterbury the previous year. They made numerous visits to the houses of Edward's local friends and relations and Cassandra stayed on when the others returned to Steventon in October so that when Jane wrote to her during their separation, it is an indication of the busy social life in which she was involved at home.

Tom Lefroy is by no means for

gotten. Reporting a visit from Mrs. Lefroy she says:

'... *of her nephew she said nothing at all ... she did not once mention the name ... to me, and I was too proud to make any enquiries; but on my father's afterwards asking where he was, I learnt that he was gone back to London on his way to Ireland, where he is called to the Bar and means to practise.*'

She compares the pattern of life at Steventon vicarage with that at Godmersham:

'*We dine now at half after three, and have done dinner I suppose before you begin. We drink tea at half after six. I am afraid you will despise us. My father reads Cowper to us in the evening, to which I listen when I can. How do you spend your evenings? I guess that Elizabeth* [their brother's wife]

Deane House from Deane churchyard. This was home to the Harwood family, who often invited their friends, the Austens, to visit and to attend the balls they gave in their elegant mansion.

works [needlework], *that you read to her, and that Edward goes to sleep.'*

She writes of dining with neighbours, and entertaining at home and of balls at Manydown and Kempshott Park. The Christmas Ball at Manydown was

'*... very thin, but by no means unpleasant. There were thirty-one people, and only eleven ladies out of the number, and but five single women in the room. Of the gentlemen present you may have some idea from the list of my partners – Mr. Wood, G. Lefroy, Rice, a Mr. Butcher (belonging to the Temples, a sailor and not of the 11th Light Dragoons), Mr. Temple (not the horrid one of all), Mr. Wm. Orde (cousin to the Kingsclere man), Mr. John Harwood, and Mr. Calland, who appeared as usual with his hat in his hand, and stood every now and then behind Catherine and me to*

be talked about and abused for not dancing. We teased him, however, into it at last ... There were twenty dances, and I danced them all, and without fatigue ...'

At Lady Dorchester's, though hardly the belle of the ball she:

'*spent a very pleasant evening, chiefly among the Manydown party. There was the same kind of supper as last year, and the same want of chairs. There were more dancers than the room could conveniently hold, which is enough to constitute a good ball at any time.*

'*I do not think I was very much in request. People were rather apt not to ask me till they could not help it; one's consequence, you know, varies so much at times without any particular reason. There was one gentleman, an officer of the Cheshire, a very good-looking young man, who, I was told,*

Steventon Church dates back to the 12th century. Here, both Jane's father and her brother James preached as rectors, followed for a short time by brother Henry until her nephew William Knight was ready to take over the living. Beside the church was the home of the Digweeds, but the ancient manor house was destroyed in a 20th-century fire and only a Victorian block of servants' quarters survives.

wanted very much to be introduced to me; but as he did not want it quite enough to take much trouble in effecting it, we never could bring it about ...'

The mother of writer Mary Russell, whose family had been at the rectory before the Lefroys and then lived in nearby Alresford, described Jane Austen to her daughter as 'the prettiest, silliest, most affected, husband-hunting butterfly'. Cousin Eliza reported that

Jane and Cassandra were 'perfect beauties, and of course gain hearts of dozens'. We can imagine Jane, just 23, as lively, attractive and flirtatious. A clerical friend of Mrs. Lefroy, the Rev. Samuel Blackall, was eager to make her better acquaintance at this time but his pomposity ruled out any hope of Jane being interested in a proposal. It is frustrating that we have no satisfactory portrait of her. Cassandra made a sketch (see page 7) from which an engraving was made for Edward Austen-Leigh's 1870 *A Memoir of Jane Austen* but it was only guardedly endorsed by the Austen relations so cannot be considered a good likeness. Brother Henry, in a biographical note published with *Northanger Abbey*, and written after her death, gave a more staid picture:

'Of personal attractions she possessed a considerable share. Her stature was that of true elegance. It could have been increased without exceeding the middle height. Her carriage and deportment were quiet, yet graceful. Her features were separately good. Their assemblage produced an unrivalled expression of the cheerfulness, sensibility, and benevolence, which were her real characteristics. Her complexion was of the finest texture. It might with truth be said, that her eloquent blood spoke through her modest cheek.'

This, perhaps, is Jane in her mature years and it certainly does not convey the true vivacity that comes through in her letters and novels.

In the spring of 1799, Jane was again enjoying the lively atmosphere of Bath. Edward Austen-Leigh was being troubled by incipient gout and had decided to try the waters as a cure. Accompanied by his wife and two eldest children, his mother and Jane, he took a house in Queen Square. The following year, while Cassandra was on a visit to Godmersham and Jane was staying with the Lloyds at Ibthorpe after attending a ball, their parents decided to abandon Steventon and retire to Bath. The Rev. Austen was 70, but the decision seems to have been a sudden one for there had been plans to alter the Steventon garden. It is said that when Jane arrived back home, accompanied by Martha Lloyd, she was greeted by the news and promptly fainted with shock.

The interior of Steventon church.

BATH

Jane Austen had certainly enjoyed the shops, the entertainments and social life of her previous visits to Bath but she was very attached to the Hampshire home where she was born and grew up. Though she may not have had so strong an aversion to the city as her character Anne Elliot in *Persuasion* who persisted 'in a very determined, very silent, disinclination for Bath', she was not entirely happy with the move. James was set to take over his father's duties but he already had a well established household, and since the cost of transporting furniture and effects to Bath would be high it was decided to sell or leave behind many of their possessions. These included 500 books from the library and Jane's own pianoforte.

Jane tried her best to be enthusiastic about the imminent removal, putting on a brave front as soon as she had recovered from the news. By the beginning of 1801 she is writing to Cassandra:

'My mother looks forward with as much certainty as you can do, to our keeping two maids – my father is the only one not in the secret. We plan having a steady cook, and a young giddy house-maid, with a sedate, middle-aged man, who is to undertake the double office of husband to the former and sweetheart to the latter. No children of course to be allowed on either side ...

'My mother bargains for having no trouble at all in furnishing our house in Bath – and I have engaged for your willingly undertaking to do it all. I get more and more reconciled to the idea of our removal. We have lived long enough in this neighbourhood, the Basingstoke balls are

Pulteney Bridge and the Avon. The crescent of buildings just below the church on the hill is the Paragon.

Arriving in Bath.
'*When Lady Russell ... was entering Bath on a wet afternoon, and driving through the long course of streets from the Old Bridge to Camden-place, amidst the dash of other carriages, the heavy rumble of carts and drays, the bawling of newsmen, muffin-men and milkmen, and the ceaseless clink of pattens, she made no complaint. No, these were noises which belonged to the winter pleasures; her spirits rose under their influence; and, like Mrs. Musgrove, she was feeling, though not saying, that, after being long in the country, nothing could be so good for her as a little quiet cheerfulness.*
'*Anne did not share these feelings. She persisted in a very determined, though very silent, disinclination for Bath; caught the first dim view of the extensive buildings, smoking in rain, without any wish of seeing them better; felt their progress through the streets to be, however, disagreeable, yet too rapid; for who would be glad to see her when she arrived? And looked back, with fond regret, to the bustles of Uppercross and the seclusion of Kellynch.*'
Persuasion

FAR LEFT
The Paragon. Uncle James Leigh Perrot and his wife had lodgings at number 1 on the slope above Walcot Street and the Avon. Jane Austen came to stay with them there.

LEFT
Laura Place, an address which Jane Austen thought would be far too expensive for the family!

BELOW
The Countess of Huntingdon's chapel in the Paragon.

Mrs Elton on the attractions of Bath
in *Emma*:

'... *where the waters do agree, it is
quite wonderful the relief they give.
In my Bath life, I have seen such
instances of it! and it is so cheerful
a place, that it could not fail of being
of use to M. Woodhouse's spirits ...
And as to its recommendations to
you, I fancy I need not take much
pains to dwell on them. The advantages of Bath to the young are pretty
generally understood. It could be a
charming introduction for you, who
have lived so secluded a life; and I
could immediately secure you some
of the best society in the place.*'

*certainly on the decline, there is something
interesting in the bustle of going away, and
the prospect of spending future summers
by the sea or in Wales is very delightful ...
It must not be generally known, however,
that I am not sacrificing a great deal in
quitting the country – or I can expect to
inspire no tenderness, no interest in those
we leave behind.*'

Where in Bath were they to live? 'In
what part of Bath do you mean to place
your bees?' writes Jane to Cassandra.
'We are afraid of the South Parade's
being too hot.'

At the beginning of May, Jane and
Mrs. Austen went to stay with the
Leigh Perrots in the Paragon in Bath to
begin their hunt for a house. Mr.
Austen went off to visit Edward in Kent
and then to London and Cassandra visited the Lloyds at Ibthorpe and the
Fowles at Kintbury, so deciding where
to live was largely left to them.

Jane wasted no time in beginning the
search. The day after her arrival she
walked to the Pump Room with her

uncle and looked at two houses in
Green Park Buildings on the way back,
'one of which pleased me very well'. A
week later she attended the last ball of
the season:

'*I dressed myself as well as I could, and
had all my finery much admired at home.
By nine o'clock my uncle, aunt and I
entered the rooms and linked Miss
Winstone on to us. Before tea it was rather
a dull affair; but then before tea did not
last long, for there was only one dance,
danced by four couple. Think of four couple,
surrounded by about an hundred people,
dancing in the Upper Rooms at Bath!*

'*After tea we cheered up; the breaking
up of private parties sent some scores more
to the ball, and tho' it was shockingly and
inhumanly thin for this place, there were
people enough to have made five or six very
pretty Basingstoke assemblies ...*'

The tail end of the season was not
providing the glamour and excitement
which one might expect of a fashionable
spa and which would have added con-
siderably to the social round. The night

after the ball was even more disappointing:

'Another stupid party ... perhaps, if larger they might be less intolerable, but here there were only just enough to make one card table, with six people to look on and talk nonsense to each other.'

Then came news of the sale of their possessions at Steventon rectory: eight guineas for tables, eight for Jane's pianoforte and sixty one and a half for three cows being some compensation for the low figure raised by the furniture; and their books apparently sold well too. Their severance from the old home now felt final. The search for the new one continued: 'The houses in the streets near Laura Place I should expect to be above our price,' Jane wrote to Cassandra, and it was at the opposite end of Great Pulteney Street, in Sydney Terrace, facing Sydney Gardens that they eventually took a house. Sydney Gardens, on the opposite side of the Avon from the centre of town, was then on the outskirts and

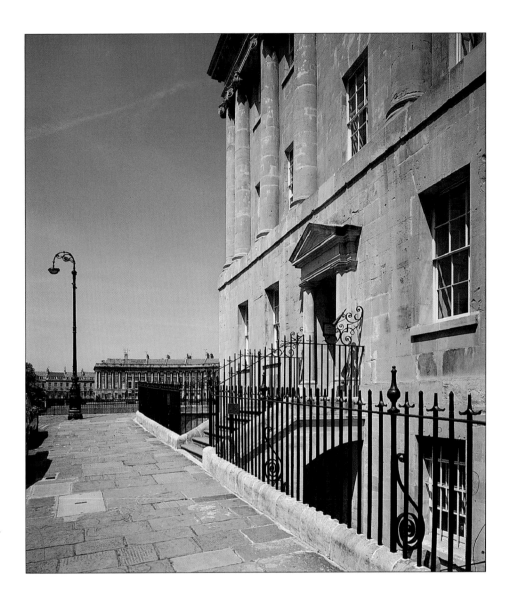

Royal Crescent, by John Wood the Younger, dates from 1767. It forms a 180-metre (600-foot) elipse of 30 houses, its 114 Ionic columns beneath a single cornice.

Queen's Square, where Edward Austen took number 13 in 1799 and Jane and her mother spent a midsummer holiday with him. It was built by John Wood the elder as his first great project in Bath, beginning in 1729. Jane found the view 'far more cheerful than the Paragon.'

RIGHT
14 Alfred Street. The iron balconies, railings and lamp holder at the entrance, with snuffers for the linkman's torches on either side, are typical of Bath.

overlooked open countryside. The Austens rented the house from the end of May 1801 and the family was reunited there in June.

Bath, when Jane Austen knew it, was no longer the highly fashionable resort it had been when Sheridan set his sparkling comedies there. The Prince Regent's interest in Brighton had made it more attractive to fashionable society since he had had the Royal Pavilion built in 1782 (rebuilding it in its present oriental style in 1817). It was closer to London and offered the diversions of a seaside town. Bath was fast becoming a health spa rather than a pleasure resort. It was a centre of solid respectability, eminently suitable for retirement homes for clergymen such as the Rev. Austen. A fitting resort for

the older generation, though still offering many attractions for the younger relatives who might visit or accompany them, it was no longer the magnet for the highly sophisticated upper classes which it had been when Beau Nash presided as the main arbiter of taste.

Bath takes its name from a bathing place fed by the hot springs which still bubble out of the earth beneath the modern Pump Room. Since long before the Romans came to Britain, the waters have seeped down through the earth where they have been heated to a temperature of 46.5 C (120 F) before being forced upwards and emerging at the rate of about 1,137,000 litres (250,000 gallons) a day. Here, where the mineral-laden water stained the earth red and where considerable heat was produced even when the land was frozen solid in winter, the Celts of Iron Age Britain worshipped their sun god Sul.

Legend has it that the discovery that water from Sul's spring had healing

Abbey Square with the façade of the Pump Room on the left. The Greek inscription on the architrave can be translated 'Water is best'.

properties was made about 500 B.C. by a prince called Bladud, according to legend the father of Shakespeare's King Lear, who was banished from court for being a leper. Farmers in the Avon valley took pity on him and gave him work as a swineherd. One day he noticed that some of his pigs, who were affected with a skin disease, were wallowing in the hot mud around the spring to emerge suddenly cured. He too, entered the muddy waters and his leprosy was cured. He returned to his father's court and, when he in turn became king, founded a city where the springs rose from the earth.

City or not, the mineral springs were known long before the Romans arrived following the invasion by the armies of the Emperor Claudius in A.D. 43. When the Romans came they probably set up a military fort by the loop of the Avon where the trackway from Wales to London and the ancient Fosse Way crossed. But with their realization of the benign medicinal properties of Aquae Sulis an important centre was born with recreational baths on a major scale. By the last quarter of the first century, Bath had its first stone buildings. The Roman city was not large – about 9 hectares (22 acres) and everything was dwarfed by the baths, which were the largest of their kind in western Europe. There were three great plunge and swimming baths. The largest, now

OPPOSITE
Bath Abbey.
There was a Benedictine monastery here in Saxon times followed after the Norman conquest by the huge cathedral. The present church, no bigger than the Norman nave, dates from the beginning of the 16th century.

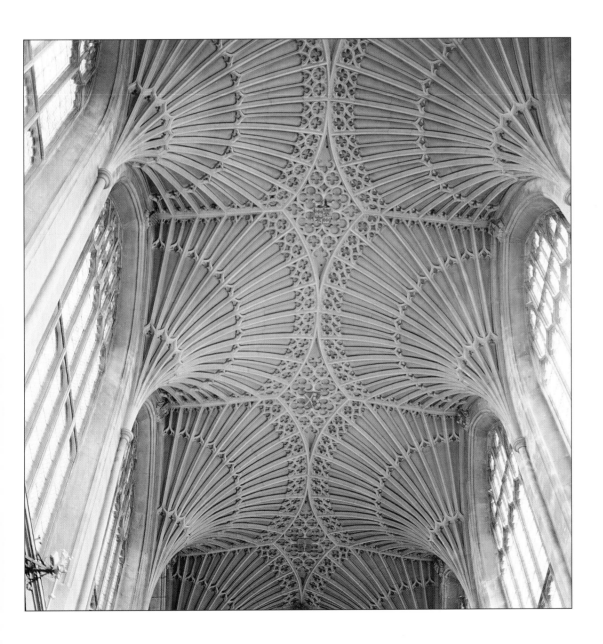

The fan-vaulted roof of Bath Abbey.

OPPOSITE
The Great Bath, the heart of the
ancient bath complex. The pillars
and statues above the parapet are
late 19th century work, not Roman.
Only the square pillar bases
and the bath itself are ancient
though the lead lining of the bath
itself survives.

the Great Bath, was at first open to the air with alcoved colonnades, but later it was roofed by a great tunnel vault with a span of over 10 metres (35 feet) with open lunettes at each end to allow steam to escape. Later, there were hot baths of the hammam type at both ends of the building, though it is not known whether there were any included in the original building.

The Celtic goddess Sul became assimilated with the Roman Minerva and as Sul-Minerva became the presiding spirit of the temple. Its pediment with a disc bearing the head of Sul surrounded by Gorgon-like hair or flames and the flowing robes of the supporting Victories makes this the masterpiece of Romano-Celtic sculpture in Britain. It was supported on columns with fine-cut capitals and entablature and there was a restrainedly beautiful cult statue of the goddess of which the gilded-bronze head survives. One votive dedication discovered in the excavations suggests that Gallic sculptors were among those working here for it bears the inscription of a stone-mason from the neighbourhood of Chartres in modern France. Many other fine examples of provincial Roman art have been found in Bath. Among them are figured panels of the four seasons, a coping depicting a mastiff biting a stag, a pewter candelabra in the form of a stag and a pewter figure of a water deity with a painted beard and moustache, similar to the shield of the pediment bearing an ambiguous head of what is possibly Sul-Minerva but which might perhaps be another deity.

It was not only work that brought foreign artists and craftsman to Bath. The spa attracted pilgrims and those seeking to be healed of their bodily ills. Excavations enable the modern visitor to see the sacrificial altar sited on the precinct of the temple, and the steps which led up to the temple itself. In the museum can be seen the votive offerings, coins, inscriptions, memorials and artefacts which were found. Almost nothing of this was known to Jane Austen. It had lain buried for more than a thousand years. Workmen digging a

The entrance to the King's and
Queen's Baths.

RIGHT
A carving of a river or sea god
found on the temple site.

sewer in Stall Street had unearthed the head of the statue of Sul-Minerva in 1727 and more discoveries were made in the 1750s; but it was not until 1878 that the city engineer, investigating a leak under the King's Bath, discovered the great Roman Bath, still lined with lead from the Mendip Hills. Lead was a metal with which the Romans were familiar but in Bath they found an unusual mineral, a curious black fuel burning on the altars of the goddess 'which did not waste away but turned to

LEFT
The Great Bath was probably used
for both immersion and swimming.
The stone platform (left foreground)
makes an effective diving board.

stony lumps': Somerset cannel coal.

Rome withdrew many of its legions from Britain after A.D. 383 and by 410 Britain had ceased to be part of the Roman Empire. Aquae Sulis was by then fortified with a defensive wall, built towards the end of the Roman period: but the pattern of Roman life had begun to disintegrate, though it was not until 550 that Aquae Sulis was engulfed by the spread of the invading Saxons. A change towards a wetter climate was responsible for flooding the baths and, with the withdrawal of the Romans, there would have been no experienced engineers sufficiently capable of carrying out repairs to structural damage which led to the sinking of masonry and cracking of columns. The once famous watering place became buried beneath layers of earth and the fine Roman town forgotten.

The hot springs were rediscovered in the 12th century and, by the 16th century, three baths were in use: the medieval Cross Bath (in Bath Street), the nearby Hot Bath and the King's Bath by the Pump Room. Those with skin complaints used the Cross Bath: the King's Bath tended to be more frequented by gentlefolk.

It was the visit of Anne of Denmark, the consort of James I, early in the 17th century which began the development of Bath as an increasingly popular resort for the rich and ailing. The waters were being recommended for drinking as well as bathing – the royal physician at the court of Charles II even prescribed them. In the same reign, diarist Samuel Pepys, who tried the waters in 1668, saw the crowd of people in the King's Bath, and thought 'it cannot be clean to go so many bodies together in the same water.'

At some point the waters gained a reputation for making barren women fertile and James II's childless queen, Mary of Modena, made a visit and spent some time in the Cross Bath, after which she conceived. There was much celebration and a pillar was erected in the centre of the bath.

A visit from Queen Anne really put Bath on the map as a fashionable venue and, during the 18th century the town rapidly expanded, its population increasing from not much more than 3,000 to ten times that amount by the time the Austens took up residence at Sydney Terrace. Not long after Queen

BELOW
Inside the Pump Room the waters
could be sampled from a fountain
in the centre of the long wall. In the
alcove to the left stands a statue of
Beau Nash above a clock made by
Thomas Tompion, who presented it
to the city in 1709, together with a
sundial to check its accuracy. The
alcove at the opposite end has a
gallery for musicians. Today, there
are sedan chairs in the room. In
Jane Austen's time the streets
would have been full of them,
a pair of chairmen, front and
rear carrying them by the shafts
to transport their client about
the town.

Anne's visit, Daniel Defoe was describing Bath as 'the resort of the sound as well as the sick, and a place that helps the indolent and the gay to commit that worst of all murders – to kill time.'

The focus of the life of fashionable Bath was a man called Richard Nash who arrived in 1705 and made a huge win of £1,000 at the gaming tables. In his 31 years he had been at Oxford, in the Guards and enrolled at the Inner Temple he had failed to achieve any distinction: but in Bath he became Master of Ceremonies for the Corporation, officiating from the time of Queen Anne through the reigns of the first two Georges.

'Beau' Nash, as he became known, made Bath synonymous with good taste and high fashion, drawing the élite of English society to take the waters and attend the balls and assemblies which he organized. He ensured that the Corporation kept the roads in good repair, the streets paved and provided with lamps. He issued licences to carriers of sedan chairs and endeavoured to control their prices; he forbad the wearing of swords inside the city, banned riding boots from the ballrooms and prohibited smoking in the public rooms as a habit disrespectful and unpleasant to the ladies. He encouraged the building of the fine Assembly Rooms and engaged an orchestra of talented musicians from London. When he died, aged 87, in 1761 he had lost most of his money through debts and lawsuits and new legislation against public gambling put an end to the lucrative profits he had made from it. But, though he died in near poverty, the city gave him a magnificent funeral, in acknowledgement of its debt to him. Novelist and playwright Oliver Goldsmith, in the biography he published the following year declared that he had 'too much merit not to become remarkable, yet too much folly to arrive at greatness'. You can see his statue in the Pump Room and next to the Theatre Royal in Sawclose is the house in which he lived. It is now a restaurant named after his mistress, Juliana Papjoy.

The increase in the number of visitors to Bath was partly due to improvements in roads and transport and in its turn justified the rebuilding of the city in a grand style providing a standard of comfort worthy of the expectations of its fashionable new residents and visitors.

A largely Elizabethan town was swept away in a building boom inspired by Richard Allen, who arrived in Bath about 1710 as an assistant in the postal service. He was responsible for developing the nationwide postal routes, making himself a fortune in the process, and bought the Combe Down quarries south of the city to provide raw material for rebuilding. London architects had declared Bath stone useless, so to prove them wrong he built his own house in York Street and later his mansion, Prior Park, south of Bath. He built it in the Palladian style which was greatly enhanced by the beauty of the stone. The architect for both was John Wood, a Yorkshireman, who had been in Bath since 1727 and who, with his son, was responsible for Bath's classical appearance. His first major city project was Queen Square, begun in 1729. His masterpiece, the Circus, was not started until 1754, the year he died, and was completed by his son, also called John, who continued to transform the city with developments such as Royal Crescent and the Assembly Rooms.

In 1771, Pulteney Bridge was built to the design of Robert Adam, to link the city with the new suburb of Bathwick across the river, where Sydney Gardens were laid out in 1795. It was overlooking these classical

In the Pump Room.
'Mr. Tilney did not appear. Every creature, except himself, was to be seen in the room at different periods of the fashionable hours; crowds of people were every moment passing in and out, up the steps and down; people whom nobody cared about, and nobody wanted to see; and he only was absent. "What a delightful place Bath is," said Mrs. Allen, as they sat down near the great clock, after parading the room till they were tired; "and how pleasant it would be if we had any acquaintance here." '
Northanger Abbey

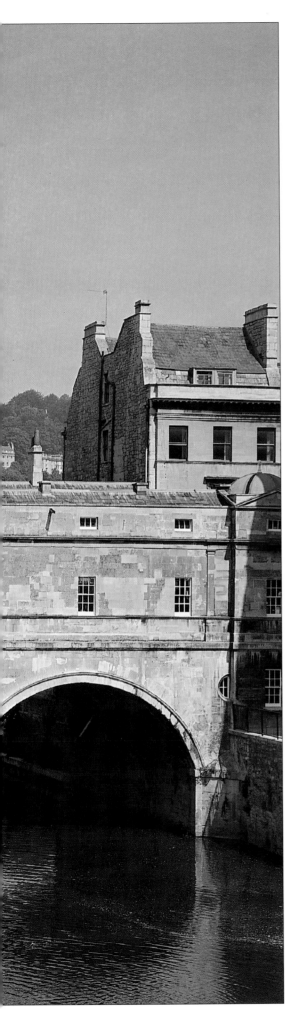

pavilions that the Austens took a house. The following year, higher up the hill above Royal Crescent, another Bath architect, John Palmer, started to build Landsdowne Crescent.

Bath at its zenith was the setting for plays by Richard Brinsley Sheridan, and novels by Tobias Smollett and Henry Fielding. Its heyday was long past when Jane Austen knew it and in describing some of its inhabitants she is gently critical of those who are not *quite* from the top drawer of fashion as they imagine themselves to be.

In several of her novels Bath plays a peripheral role and in two it is the main location. It is here that she sets more than half of *Northanger Abbey*, although, in its early form as *Susan*, it was probably written before her visit to Edward's family in 1799. She would no doubt have already heard much about life there and amendments based on her own experience may have been made before it was first offered for publication in 1803 to Crosby and Son. It was sold

ABOVE
The Circus, dating from 1745, was John Wood's masterpiece: it is 97 metres (318 ft) across, and built in three sections, each of eleven houses. The façades are embellished with tiers of Doric, Ionic and Corinthian columns and a frieze on the entablature of the ground floor tier features 365 motifs symbolizing the arts and sciences.

LEFT
Pulteney Bridge, built to the design of Robert Adam in 1771, links the centre of the city with the suburb of Bathwick with the gracious mansions at Laura Place (where Lady Dalrymple lived in *Persuasion*) via Great Pulteney Street (where Catherine Morland stays with the Allens in *Northanger Abbey)*, to Sydney Gardens where the Austens decided to make their Bath home.

The New, or Upper Assembly Rooms were built by John Wood the Younger between 1769-71. They consist of two elegant blocks on Bennet Street and Alfred Street with the octagonal card room and antechambers between them, with the entrance portico and vestibule on the open piazza to the west. Harrison's Rooms, on the site of what are now the Parade Gardens between the Abbey and the River Avon, were the original Assembly Rooms, where Beau Nash presided. Jane Austen knew them as the Lower Rooms. Their prestige declined after the opening of the new Upper Rooms in 1771. The Upper Rooms are still the setting for balls, concerts and public events, as they were 200 years ago. They were restored by the National Trust in the 1930s, re-opened in 1938 but were gutted by incendiary bombs during one of the heavy air raids on Bath during the Second World War. Restored to their former magnificence with their original chandeliers, which had fortunately been in store elsewhere during the war, they re-opened in 1963, the basement areas being turned into a Museum of Costume.

OPPOSITE
Sally Lunn's house (1482), the oldest in Bath, although its façade dates only from the 17th century.

RIGHT
Milsom Street, with Beechen Cliff in the distance. Then as now it was a smart shopping street. In *Northanger Abbey* the Tilneys lived there, while Edgar's Buildings, where Jane Austen's Thorpes had their home, faces its top end on the other side of George Street.

for £10, the arrangement being made by a Mr. Seymour, probably an associate of Henry Austen, who was placing the book on his sister's behalf. The publisher advertised it as a two-volume novel but it never appeared – perhaps he saw Jane's parody of the gothick novel, examples of which already featured strongly in his list, as an attack on the genre which was best suppressed.

There was great disappointment, even resentment, that it did not appear.

When, nearly ten years after her residence in Bath she wrote *Persuasion*, she set almost all the story in the city, creating a picture of life there which shows how clearly she remembered her years in the city.

Although the Austens had made their home in Bath, moving in 1804

'... the important evening came which was to usher her [Catherine] into the Upper Rooms. Her hair was cut and dressed by the best hand, her clothes put on with care... Mrs. Allen was so long in dressing, that they did not enter the room till late. The season was full, the room crowded, and the two ladies squeezed as well as they could. As for Mr. Allen, he repaired directly to the card-room, and left them to enjoy the mob by themselves. With more care for the safety of her new gown than for the comfort of her protegée, Mrs. Allen made her way through the throng of men by the door, as swiftly as the necessary caution would allow; Catherine, however, kept close at her side, and linked her arm too firmly to her friend's to be torn asunder by any common effort of a struggling assembly. But to her utter astonishment she found that to proceed along the room was by no means the way to disengage themselves from the crowd; it seemed rather to increase as they went on, whereas she had imagined that when once fairly within the door, they should easily find seats and be able to watch the dances with perfect convenience. But this was far from being the case, and though by unwearied diligence they gained even the top of the room, their situation was just the same; they saw nothing of the dancers but the high feathers of some of the ladies. Still they moved on – something better was yet in view; and by a continued exertion of strength and ingenuity they found themselves at last in the passage behind the highest bench. Here there was something less of crowd than below; and hence Miss Morland had a comprehensive view of the company beneath her, and of all the dangers of her late passage through them. It was a splendid sight and she began, for the first time that evening, to feel herself at a ball ...'
Northanger Abbey

RIGHT
Beacon Hill, the heights above the Paragon, where Jane Austen went walking on a summer day in 1799:
'We took a very charming walk from 6 to 8 up Beacon Hill, and across some fields to the village of Charlcombe, which is sweetly situated in a little green valley, as a village with such a name ought to be.'
Letter to Cassandra, 2nd June.

BELOW
Charlcombe Church dates back to Norman times and tradition says that it was once the mother church of Bath.

to 27 Green Park Buildings on the opposite side of the city, they did not spend all their time there. In the summer of 1802 they took a holiday at Dawlish and Teignmouth. In 1804 they stayed at Lyme Regis, and Jane made visits to James at Steventon, to Edward at Godmersham, to friends at Great Bookham and possibly to see her brother Frank at Ramsgate where he was in charge of raising defensive troops to face the possibility of French invasion.

During one of these holidays, Jane is thought to have formed a deep attachment to a young man whom she might have married if he had not died soon after the initial flowering of their acquaintance.

On one of her visits back to Steventon in 1802, while staying with the Bigg-Wither family at Manydown, Harris the 21-year old son of their host proposed to Jane, six years his senior, and was accepted by her. Next morning she changed her mind and insisted that her brother James drive them straight back to Bath.

The Reverend Austen and his daughters took a number of long seaside holidays during their early years in Bath. Dawlish was the planned destination for 1801 but at least part of the summer was spent at Sidmouth. Teignmouth and Starcross were other places they visited and in the summer of 1802 they went to Tenby in South Wales, making their way up to Barmouth. Louisa Lefroy seemed to think that it may have been in Sidmouth, in the summer of 1801, that Jane met a young clergyman who was staying with his brother, a doctor in the town, and they fell in love. It was agreed that he should join them later on their holiday tour but news came before this could take place that he had died. She heard this from her Aunt Cassandra who appears to have been deliberately obscure about the incident.

LEFT
An evening view of Bath from the top of Beechen Cliff on the south of the city on the other side of the Avon, where Catherine, in *Northanger Abbey*, eventually walked with Eleanor and Henry Tilney and listened to their talk of landscape painting. Although Bath is now more extensively and densely built, there was then little building on this side of the river. Today, parks and trees retain some of the feeling of space and the open countryside beyond.

In *Northanger Abbey*, Jane Austen described Beechen Cliff as: '*that noble hill, whose beautiful verdure and hanging coppice render it so striking an object from almost every opening in Bath...*'

RIGHT
Camden Crescent, which Jane Austen calls Camden Place, is high above the city, beyond the Paragon and the Upper Rooms, though within a short stroll of them.

'Sir Walter had taken a very good house in Camden-place, a lofty dignified situation, such as becomes a man of consequence ... they had the pleasure of assuring her ... undoubtedly the best in Camden-place; their drawing-rooms had many decided advantages over all the others which they had seen or heard of; and the superiority was not less in the style of the fitting-up, or the taste of the furniture. Their acquaintance was exceeding sought after. Everybody was wanting to visit them. They had drawn back from many introductions, and still were perpetually having cards left by people of whom they knew nothing.'
Persuasion

TOP FAR RIGHT
The Holburne of Menstrie Museum, in Sydney Gardens, near the Austen house in Sydney Terrace, was a tavern with a ballroom, card rooms and coffee room when Jane Austen lived in a house overlooking the gardens. These were popular pleasure gardens, with music and fireworks to enjoy on gala nights.

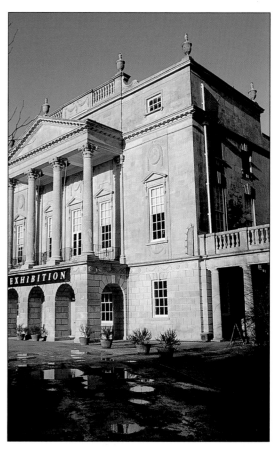

Gay Street, where Jane lived for a few months at number 25 in 1805.

The families were close, the match seemed a good one: whatever had made Jane accept, then change her mind? She had known the young man for some years, even though she may never have thought of him as a future husband. 'Single women have a dreadful propensity for being poor – which is one very strong argument in favour of matrimony,' she wrote in one of her letters and perhaps she did feel that it was time to put an end to her spinsterhood. But why the panic next day? Could it be that she bitterly remembered her experience of the previous year? She may have thought of Cassandra, who seems to have rejected the idea of marriage to anyone else after the death of Tom Lefroy, thinking that no one could measure up to him: either of these factors may have caused her to change her mind.

In Bath in 1803 or 1804, Jane began *The Watsons*, a novel with a Surrey setting which she abandoned unfinished, perhaps because of the disruption in her life at this time: perhaps because she was not satisfied with it. She does not appear to have embarked on any new work for some years, disillusioned no doubt, by the non-appearance of her novel from Crosby and Company.

The move to Green Park Buildings brought the Austens closer to the Pump Room making it more convenient for Mr. Austen to take the waters, for he was intermittently troubled by a feverish complaint and was now unable to walk without a stick. They were not to be there long for on 19 January 1805 he felt unwell and, although next morning was fit enough to breakfast with the family, he collapsed and died the following day. He was buried in the crypt of St. Swithin's, at the corner of Walcot Street and the Paragon, the church where he had been married.

Mr. Austen's death left the family income sadly depleted. To supplement what little was provided for Mrs. Austen they used the interest which Cassandra received on her bequest from Tom Lefroy: but Jane had no resources of her own. Their brothers made contributions which brought their income up to about £460 per annum: £50 each from James, Henry and Frank and the balance from Edward. They moved to 25 Gay Sreet and reduced their staff from a man and two maids to just one maid – though the house itself was in a somewhat smarter district. Martha Lloyd's mother died in April and it was arranged that she should leave Ibthorpe and become part of the household, staying with them until her marriage as second wife to Francis in 1828.

The following year the Austens resided at another address in Trim Street and in June 1806, much to Jane's satisfaction, they left the city, travelling first to Clifton, then to Adelstrop, Stoneleigh Abbey and Southampton where they stayed with brother Frank and his wife in lodgings while looking for a house that they all could share.

'They made their appearance in the Lower Rooms; and here fortune was more favourable to our heroine. The master of the ceremonies introduced to her a very gentlemanlike young man as a partner; – his name was Tilney. He seemed to be about four or five and twenty, was rather tall, had pleasing countenance, a very intelligent and lively eye, and, if not quite handsome, was very near it. His address was good, and Catherine felt herself in high luck. There was little leisure for speaking while they danced; but when they were seated at tea, she found him as agreeable as she had already given him credit for being.'
Northanger Abbey

The Lower Rooms were destroyed by a fire in 1820. They stood near North Parade where gardens now slope down to the River Avon.

BELOW
Many Bath street names are elegantly carved directly on to the dressed stone.

SOUTHAMPTON

In January 1805 Jane wrote to her brother Frank, on *H.M.S. Leopard*, which she heard was due in Portsmouth, to inform him of their father's death and a week later to tell him that their mother had found a compass and sundial among her husband's possessions which she wanted him to have as a keepsake, such astronomical instruments being of particular use to a sailor. In Ramsgate, in 1803, Frank had met a young woman called Mary Gibson and became engaged to her, though his prospects were not then secure enough to embark on marriage; but marry they did in July 1806 in Ramsgate, and they then settled in Southampton where it was decided his mother, sisters and Martha Lloyd should come to live with them, Southampton being chosen for it proximity to Portsmouth and its convenience for him when ashore.

Francis Austen, 20 months Jane's senior, had progressed well in the Royal Navy. He had seen service in home waters, the Mediterranean and the East Indies, and had had the command of ships since 1798, having been made captain in 1800. He captured a French brig off Marseilles, helped blockade Cadiz, and in 1804 was appointed to *H.M.S. Leopard*, flagship of Rear-Admiral Louis, blockading Boulogne. In 1805 he was given *H.M.S. Canopus*, again with Louis, Nelson's second-in-command. But though he met Nelson on the *Victory*, and followed him across the Atlantic in pursuit of the French fleet, Nelson decided to send the *Canopus* to

Gibraltar to take aboard water and provisions and caused Frank, much to his regret, to miss the Battle of Trafalgar. Now after taking part in the Battle of St. Domingo he was ashore, married, and waiting for a new posting.

On 10 October 1806, the Austen ladies moved into lodgings with Frank and Mary in Southampton. It took a little time to find a suitable house but they eventually decided to rent one of the largest houses in Castle Square in the north-east of the city. Their landlord was Lord Lansdowne, who had bought the square in which the remains of the keep of a Norman castle had stood, and had built for himself a turretted mansion rather like a Disneyland castle. Here he now lived with his new bride, a middle-aged, well upholstered and over-dressed Irish widow whose carriage, a phaeton was drawn by six or eight ponies

'each pair decreasing in size, and becoming lighter in colour, through all the grades of dark brown, light brown, bay and chestnut, as it was laced further from the carriage. The two leading pairs were managed by two boyish postillions.'

This is how James's son James Edward remembered them when he wrote his *Memoir* of his aunt. The comings and goings of their aristocratic neighbours and their fanciful home supplied plenty of scope for the Austen wit and sense of invention.

In February 1807, Jane wrote to Cassandra reporting that 'alterations and improvements ... advance very properly' and teasing her that if she did not come back to help with all the things they had to buy, Frank and Mary would deliberately get 'knives that will not cut, glasses that will not hold, a sofa without a seat, and a bookcase without shelves'.

There was a good size garden which ended at the old city wall which was easily accessible by steps allowing for walks along the fortifications. The garden was being
' ...put in order, by a Man who bears a remarkable good character, has a very fine complexion and asks something less than the first. The shrubs which border the gravel walk he says are only sweetbriar and roses, and the latter of an indifferent sort; – we mean to get a few of a better kind therefore, and at my own particular desire he procures us some Syringas. I could not do without a Syringa, for the sake of Cowper's Line. — We talk also of a Laburnam. — The Border under the Terrace Wall is clearing away to receive Currants and Gooseberry Bushes, and a spot is found very proper for Raspberries.'*

All was ready for them to move in on 9 March.

Even in lodgings there had been visits from the James Austens and with Frank's naval contacts there were many new people to meet. 'Our acquaintances increase too fast,' wrote Jane early in the year. As well as private entertaining there were the Assembly Rooms and a theatre in Southampton, and balls were also held in the Long Room of the Dolphin Hotel. An increasingly active social life was developing and with Mary and Martha part of the household and available to keep Mrs. Austen company, it was

The Bargate, Southampton, the north entrance to the old walled town, was built by the Normans in the 12th century. The Austen house was not far away in Castle Square.

ABOVE
Arrivals entering the public
assembly rooms before a ball. The
picture is by Rolinda Sharples
(1794-1838).

OPPOSITE
The medieval merchant's house in
French Street.

easier for Jane and Cassandra to make visits to Edward at Godmersham, Henry in London and elsewhere.

Of course there were tedious acquaintances as well as lively ones, though Jane's letters seem to place an emphasis on the former appreciating them for their comic value:

'... at seven o'clock, Mrs. Harrison, her two daughters and two Visitors, with Mr. Debary and his eldest sister walked in; and our Labour was not a great deal shorter than poor Elizabeth's [Mrs. Edward Austen had just given birth to her eleventh child], for it was past eleven before we were delivered. A second pool of Commerce, and all the longer by the addition of the two girls, who during the first had one corner of the Table and Spillikens to themselves, was the ruin of us ...'

Thus she wrote to Cassandra on 1 October 1808. A party just before Christmas seems to have been a disaster too, for it

'... produced nothing more remarkable than Miss Murden's coming too, though she had declined it absolutely in the morning, and sitting very ungraciously and very silent with us from seven o'clock till half after eleven, for so late was it, owing to the chairmen, before we got rid of them.

'The last hour, spent in a yawning and

A Ball in Southampton.

'*Our ball was rather more amusing than I expected. Martha liked it very much, and I did not gape till the last quarter of an hour. It was past nine before we were sent for, and not twelve when we returned. The room was tolerably full, and there were perhaps thirty couple of dancers. The melancholy part was to see so many dozen young women standing by without partners, and each of them with two ugly naked shoulders!*

It was the same room in which we danced fifteen years ago! I thought it all over – and in spite of the shame of being so much older [she was just short of her 33rd birthday], *felt with thankfulness that I was quite as happy now as then. We paid an additional shilling for our tea, which we took as we chose in an adjoining and very comfortable room. There were only four dances, and it went to my heart that the Miss Lances (one of them, too, named Emma!) should have partners for only two. You will not expect to hear that I was asked to dance – but I was – by the gentleman whom we met* that Sunday *with Captain d'Auvergne. We have always kept a bowing acquaintance since, and being pleased with his black eyes, I spoke to him at the ball, which brought on me this civility; but I do not know his name, and he seems so little at home in the English language, that I believe his black eyes may be the best of him ...*'
Letter to Cassandra
9th December 1808

53

The West Gate, Southampton, from inside the walls. The garden of the Austens' house was against the ancient city walls.

shivering in a wide circle around the fire, was dull enough, but the tray had admirable success. The widgeon and the preserved ginger were as delicious as one could wish.'

Only two weeks after they moved to Castle Square, Frank received the captaincy of *H.M.S. St Albans*, then at Sheerness, and consequently was not at home for the birth of his first child, Mary Jane, on 27 April. Soon he was off escorting vessels of the East India Company to China. The following year he was accompanying ships carrying troops to Portugal for the Peninsular War – and at the beginning of the next year was evacuating some of them after the Battle of Corunna and was at Spithead for their disembarkation. When he took lodgings more convenient for his duties in Yarmouth on the Isle of Wight, the Austen ladies and Martha

Lloyd were left with the large new house to themselves. It was too big and too expensive and a further move was discussed.

Edward came to the rescue. He had a suitable house near Godmersham, Kent and on his second estate near Alton, in the northern part of Hampshire there was another house which was available. They could have their choice. After much deliberation they chose Chawton Cottage in Hampshire.

In the autumn of 1808, Cassandra went to Godmersham to help her sister-in-law Elizabeth with the birth of her eleventh child, though she arrived just too late for the birth. When the baby was only ten days old, its mother died. Her eldest daughter, 15-year-old Fanny, of whom Jane was particularly fond, and the younger children were at

The Saluting Platform at Portsmouth. Jane probably went there to see her sailor brothers and their vessels. She sets part of *Mansfield Park* here.

home but the two eldest sons were at Winchester School. They were taken to stay with James's children at Steventon and then to Southampton before returning to school.

Despite the sadness surrounding their visit Jane found her nephews engaging company, taking them on excursions, playing games of spillikins, bilboquet and cards, telling riddles and conundrums, making paper ships and bombarding them with horse-chestnuts brought from Steventon.

'*We had a little water party yesterday; I and my two nephews went from the Itchen Ferry up to Northam, where we landed, looked into the 74 [naval vessel with 74 guns], and walked home ... I had not proposed doing more than cross the Itchen ... but it proved so pleasant, and so much to the satisfaction of all, that when we reached the middle of the stream we agreed to be rowed up the river; both the boys rowed great part of the way, and their questions and remarks, as well as their enjoyment, were very amusing ...*'

Netley Abbey, though they did not reach it on that occasion, was a favourite excursion, whether by water or by foot and ferry: a comfortable five kilometres (three miles) there and back. Another favourite walk was along the old town walls which edged the bottom of the Castle Square garden.

Jane seems to have liked the Southampton neighbourhood but the move to yet another new home after only two years does not seem to have disturbed her, once she knew that they were returning to the Hampshire countryside. Meanwhile, she determined to make the most of Southampton's attractions. At the beginning of December she wrote to

Cassandra:

'A larger circle of acquaintance and an increase of amusement is quite in character with our approaching removal. Yes – I mean to go to as many Balls as possible, that I may have a good bargain. Everybody is very much concerned at our going away, and everybody is acquainted with Chawton and speaks of it as a remarkably pretty village; and everybody knows the House we describe ...'

There was one last ball in Southampton at the end of January:

'We were very well entertained, and could have staid longer but for the arrival of my List shoes to convey me home, and I did not like to keep them waiting in the cold. The room was tolerably full, and the Ball opened by Miss Glyn; the Miss Lances had partners, Capt. D'Auvergne's friend appeared in regimentals, Caroline Maitland had an officer to flirt with, and Mr. John Harrison was deputed by Capt. Smith, being himself absent, to ask me to dance. Everything went well you see, especially after we had tucked Mrs. Lance's neckerchief in behind, and fastened it with a pin.'

The anticipated return to a country home seems to have stimulated Jane's interest in writing again. Shortly before departing Castle Square, under the pseudonym Mrs. Ashton Davies, she wrote to Crosby and Company enquiring after the still unpublished *Susan* and offering a copy of the manuscript should the original have been lost and declaring that if the offer were unacceptable she would feel at liberty to offer the book elsewhere. Crosby wrote back that his company was not bound to publish the book but would take action if anyone else did, though she could buy back the manuscript for the same sum they had paid for it: £10.

Admiral Horatio Nelson's flagship *H.M.S. Victory*, on which he died at the battle of Trafalgar, in its dry dock in Portsmouth naval dockyard which features in *Mansfield Park*. Francis Austen served under Nelson and narrowly missed being at Trafalgar.

CHAWTON

Chawton Cottage was chosen for the Austen ladies' new home partly because the widowed Edward would in future be able to spend at least part of the year at Chawton Manor House, though it had been let until 1812. Another reason was that Henry had established a branch of his banking firm at Alton and his business would take him there. More particularly, perhaps, the balance of choice was tipped by a general affection for Hampshire – 'the Hampshire-born Austens' Jane called their branch of the family – and relative proximity to their old home and friends around Steventon,

Chawton Cottage, Jane Austen's house from July 1809. This is the garden side of the house.

'Chawton' Cottage, Jane Austen's home from July 1809. The front door opens straight into the living room. Edward had the window to the left blocked and turned into a bookcase, opening up a new window on the side wall.

where James still lived. They may also have thought that being on Edward's doorstep at Godmersham they would have been too drawn into the life of the big house rather than being able to revolve in a milieu of their own choice.

Chawton is a small village about a kilometre and a half (one mile) southwest of the town of Alton on the road to Winchester. The cottage, which had formerly been tenanted by Edward Austen's steward, was larger than the word suggests. Standing at the end of the village street, it was near the junction of the road to Gosport with the road from Southampton and Winchester to London. Indeed, it may

previously have been a coaching inn. A large pond (now drained) was set in the angle between the roads which carried a considerable amount of traffic. One of Jane's nieces later remembered how comforting it was 'to have the awful stillness of night frequently broken by the sound many of passing carriages, which seemed sometimes even to shake the bed': not a sentiment which most people would share today, but even Mrs. Austen seemed to have enjoyed the frequent traffic on the road outside.

Once the decision to come to Chawton had been made, the move could not be immediate but some changes were put in hand. Both sitting-

rooms had windows looking out onto the road, and that of the large room to the left of the front door was blocked up and the space turned into a bookcase, a new window being cut in the side wall to look out over turf and trees towards the fence and hedge which hid the Winchester road. The garden is smaller today but the house does not appear to be greatly changed.

At the beginning of December Jane was writing to Cassandra:
'We want to be settled at Chawton in time for Henry to come to us for some shooting, in October at least; not a little earlier, and Edward may visit us after taking his boys back to Winchester [at the start of the autumn term]; *suppose we name the 4th of September?'*

She was looking forward to the move, determined to buy a piano instead of renting one as she had in Bath and Southampton ' ... as good a one as can be got for thirty guineas, and I will practise country dances, that we may have some amusement for out nephews and nieces, when we have the pleasure of their company.' Mrs. Knight saw the bachelor rector of Chawton as a marriage prospect for Jane and she joked back 'depend upon it that I *will* marry Mr. Papillon, whatever may be his reluctance or my own.'

In fact they moved in in July, after

Chawton Cottage, the general living-room. Here Jane Austen is thought to have written many of her novels, probably working on the table with a sheet of blotting paper under which she could quickly hide the page if someone, unaware of her writing, surprised her. She wrote on small sheets of paper, folding ordinary sheets of writing paper in half until she had a number of them to make fascicles of 32, 48 or 80 pages, stitched to form small booklets to give her a sense of her novel coming into being.

Water for tea was heated in a copper kettle on the grate hob. The cupboards to the left of the fireplace were used for storing groceries such as tea and sugar which it was Jane's responsibility to order.

Chawton Cottage, the drawing-room. The pianoforte is similar to the one Jane Austen owned. She began each day with piano practice.

the month Frank and Mary's first son was born and Jane wrote a congratulatory verse which read:

'As for ourselves, we're very well;
As unaffected prose will tell. –
Cassandra's pen will paint our state,
The many comforts that await
Our Chawton home, how much we find
Already in it, to our mind;
And how convinced, that when complete
It will all other Houses beat
That ever have been made or mended,
With rooms concise, or rooms distended.
You'll find us very snug next year,
Perhaps with Charles and Fanny near,
For now it often does delight us
To fancy them just over-right us.'

There were six bedrooms, enough to house visiting relations, though Jane and Cassandra probably shared a bedroom. The building is an L-shape, the longer arm parallel with the road. The room to the right, looking from the road, was entered directly from the street. Here, a few months after they moved in, a traveller passing the window in a post-chaise reported to Mrs. Knight that he had seen 'the Chawton party looking very comfortable at breakfast'.

This is the room in which Jane was to return to her writing and much of her published work was written or revised here, on her mahogany desk by the front door or even on the dining-table. Though callers could see her writing through the window she insisted that the creaky door leading to the rest of the house should not be oiled so that she would have some warning of people coming in and could slip her writing out of sight under her blotting paper, thus keeping her writing a secret from strangers. The other front room, with its blocked window, was the more

Chawton Cottage. The bedroom which Jane Austen used, or perhaps shared with her sister Cassandra.

formal drawing-room. Upstairs, Jane's room was on the left at the top of the stairs; her mother had the room across the corridor with two large windows looking out onto the road. There were dormer-windowed rooms above and more rooms in the rear wing for Martha, the servants and visitors. There was a well in the yard behind and beyond that a bakehouse with an oven and a wash-boiler.

At Chawton, Cassandra and Jane became increasingly responsible for running the household. Mrs. Austen, now 70, devoted herself mainly to needlework and gardening. When both daughters were at home it was Jane's responsibility to make breakfast and to order tea, sugar and wine stores. Cassandra took care of everything else.

When Jane came down in the morning she would start the day by practising on her piano so as not to disturb the others later on. She would then put the kettle on and make breakfast. There were rustic benches in the garden for when they preferred to sit outside but in the afternoon, weather permitting, she and Cassandra would usually go for a walk, to shop in Alton, to visit a neighbour or to simply enjoy the countryside.

Chawton House – the 'Great House' as the Austens called it, is only a short way along the road towards Winchester. It is approached by a drive through its parkland, almost opposite the vicarage where the Papillons lived and who soon became friends, as did the Middletons who had the Great House on lease before Edward began to live there himself. Set in the park alongside the Great House is the church of St. Nicholas where the family regularly

RIGHT
The approach and Chawton House.

BELOW
Chawton House. An Elizabethan house set in parkland, this was owned by Jane Austen's uncle and then by her brother Edward whom he adopted as his heir. When Jane knew the house, its stone walls were hidden beneath a layer of painted stucco.

worshipped and where Mrs. Austen and Cassandra were buried. Further in this direction and to the east is Upper Farringdon where the Rev. John Benn was rector. His daughter became a family friend and even had the first part of the newly published *Pride and Prejudice* read aloud to her at Chawton, though without the secret of its authorship being revealed.

Alton, not much more than ten minutes' walk from Chawton Cottage, would have been visited frequently for shopping. It still has many 18th-century frontages which Jane would have known, sometimes concealing much older buildings. There were old inns around the square and a church with a Norman nave and tower complete with amusing animal carvings. There was a skirmish here during the Civil War in

which a Royalist colonel was shot while standing by the pulpit: there are lead bullets still embedded in the tower. Close by, too, is Wyards Farm, where Jane's niece Anna came to live with her husband Ben Lefroy. But walks did not have to be combined with a visit or linked to a useful purpose; they could be taken for their own sake, in the woods of Chawton Park across the meadows and along the lanes of this charming countryside that Jane Austen loved.

Since they had neither horses nor carriage – though later there was a donkey cart, excursions on their own were restricted to within walking distance. For longer expeditions they relied on friends or family providing transportation. Cost, and the unsuitability of ladies travelling alone, prevented them from making too much use of public coaches or privately-hired carriages, but nevertheless, there were frequent visits to distant friends and relations.

At Chawton, Jane again took out her old novel, *Elinor and Marianne,* and began to rewrite it. We do not know what prompted her to do so. Perhaps the more relaxed atmosphere of country life re-awakened her creative urge, or maybe the negative behaviour of Richard Crosby and Company stimulated her to show them she *would* be published. However, according to Henry Austen, the family had some difficulty persuading her to publish the book that resulted: *Sense and Sensibility.* Henry placed it with Thomas Egerton of the Military Library, with an office in Whitehall, London, and probably advanced her the cost of publication. The arrangement was that she would pay the publishing costs and have the receipts less a commission to the publisher for handling publication. She was so sure that receipts would not cover the costs that she planned her accounts

The church of St. Nicholas, Chawton was remodelled by Victorian 'improvers'. The chancel and sanctuary are all that remain of the church where Mr. Papillon and Jane's brother Henry preached. The graves of Mrs. Austen and of Cassandra are in the churchyard.

in anticipation of a loss. To her suprise it made her a profit of £140. By April 1811 she was in London correcting proofs and the book was published that November. By then she was well into writing *Mansfield Park* but the success of *Sense and Sensibility* led her to put that aside to revise *First Impressions*, which was sold to Egertons outright for £110. Its author had hoped to get £150 but probably accepted the smaller sum to avoid giving Henry further trouble. It was published in January 1813 as *Pride and Prejudice* and gained excellent reviews.

In April 1813, Henry's wife Eliza died after a long and painful illness and Henry drove down to Chawton to take Jane back with him to London where she stayed for a few weeks, keeping him company and comforting him in his bereavement. She was back at Chawton in July when Edward and his family took possession of the Great House which had by that time been vacated by its tenants. In September she accompanied them back to Godmersham, though by then she had probably finished writing *Mansfield Park* which draws upon her experience of life in a big country house. Some of the people she met provided prototypes for characters in her next book, *Emma*, which she began in January at Chawton. She also made a trip to London in March when she possibly worked on the proofs of *Mansfield Park* which was published in May. (On the way from Chawton Henry read or had read to him the first part of either proofs or manuscript.) That August, brother Charles's wife died following the birth of her fourth child.

Emma was finished by the end of March 1815, inspired by a visit to her godfather at Great Bookham and an excursion to Box Hill. *Mansfield Park*

had sold out but Egerton decided against issuing a second edition. Consequently a new publisher was sought and Henry began negotiations with John Murray. Murray was only willing to pay £450 and to have the copyright of the two earlier books included. The bargaining was interrupted when Henry became seriously ill but it was finally agreed that the books would be published at the author's expense, less a ten per cent commission to John Murray.

Jane was in London looking after her brother and so met his doctor who also attended the Prince Regent. Through him she was able to visit Carlton House, the Prince Regent's residence, and was invited by the royal librarian to dedicate her next book to the Prince. Since she disapproved of

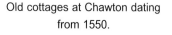
Old cottages at Chawton dating from 1550.

him she was not inclined to do so, until it was made clear that she did not have a great deal of choice in the matter. This had the effect of stirring a rather lethargic publisher into action and the book came out in December 1815 (though it bears the date 1816) and was well received. In London at the beginning of the month, awaiting its publication, she marked up revisions to the second edition of *Mansfield Park*, minor changes including new details in the Portsmouth scenes. This appeared in February 1816, but was a commercial failure.

Henry had recovered from his illness but was now beset by business worries of a much more disastrous kind. His bank collapsed and at the beginning of March he and his partners were declared bankrupt. His brother Edward lost £2,000, Mr Leigh Perrot £10,000, Charles Austen 'hundreds', and many other investors, including Henry's servants, lost smaller sums. Jane lost the profits from her writing which the bank was holding. The rich relations seem to have been able to absorb these losses and Henry himself began a new life by taking Holy Orders, being by the end of the year installed as curate to Papillon at Chawton. Charles had some further bad luck when his ship

Alton, the nearby town to which Jane Austen would walk to do her shopping. It still has many fine old inns and houses.

Phoenix was lost in a gale off Asia Minor and though the crew were saved he was faced with court martial.

Work on *Persuasion* had already begun at Chawton early in August 1815 and continued, but Jane's health was troubling her. She was tired and depressed and had rheumatic pains in her back. There were sometimes strange dark and light patches on her skin and the family's current problems did not help matters. At the end of April 1816, Cassandra took her to Cheltenham in the hope that the spa waters would alleviate her condition. They broke the journey at Steventon and at Kintbury, where Mary Jane Fowle later remembered that Jane 'went over the old places and recalled old recollections associated with them in a very particular manner' as if 'she never expected to see them again'.

Back at Chawton *Persuasion* was again resumed and completed, with some final rewriting of the penultimate chapter and parts of others. Henry had finally managed to recover *Susan* from Crosby, and Jane began to think of revising it, changing the heroine's name to Catherine, for another novel of the same name had appeared in 1809.

In September she was feeling sufficiently recovered for Cassandra to accompany James's ailing wife to Cheltenham. Jane was strong enough to spend a day at Alton and walk home by moonlight, but complained of her increased household responsibilities: *'Composition seems to me impossible, with a head full of joints of mutton and doses of rhubarb.'*

By the New Year she was developing ideas for another novel set in a seaside town, Sanditon, which was originally going to be called *The Brothers*. In the middle of March, Jane confided in her niece Fanny that 'Miss Catherine is put upon the shelve for the present ... but I have something ready for Publication, which may perhaps appear about a twelvemonth hence.'

On occasions when she was too weak to go out walking, Jane would take drives in her mother's donkey cart; to avoid the bother that all that involved she informed Fanny that she was going to ride the donkey. She had a saddle made and on 22 March enjoyed her first ride, with Edward and Cassandra walking beside her and Jane looking forward to repeating the experience. Any improvement was short-lived. A relapse seems to have been brought about by the death of Mr. Leigh Perrot, her mother's brother, and her concern at the discovery that his will did not make provision for Mrs. Austen as they had all expected.

Twelve chapters of the new book had been written before illness forced her to lay down her pen. She was tired, her muscles weak, and to abdominal pains were added nausea, vomiting and diarrhoea. From 13 April she abandoned her bed only to transfer to a sofa. There were periods when she felt better, when her head cleared and she had less pain, though she was feverish at night and tired during the day. But on 27 April she felt it was time to make her will: Cassandra was to inherit everything except for small bequests of £50 to Henry and £50 to his French housekeeper, who had lost her savings in his bankruptcy. Later she added a gold chain for her goddaughter Louisa Knight and a lock of hair for Fanny.

The Alton doctor was able to do little for her and, placing their confidence in a Winchester physician, Dr. Lyford, it was decided that she would be better there, where he would be on hand to afford her regular treatment.

OPPOSITE
Selborne, home of famous naturalist Gilbert White is only a short distance from Chawton. He lived here at The Wakes.

VISITS

The Austen family had connections in several parts of the country. George Austen had come from a Kentish family and they still had relatives there. His uncle and benefactor Francis had by 1743 become rich enough to buy the Red House in Sevenoaks. Jane visited her great-uncle there in 1788, when she was 12 years old. Her father's second cousin, Thomas Knight, who adopted Jane's brother Edward as his heir, lived at Godmersham Park, about 13 kilometres (eight miles) southwest from Canterbury on the road to Ashford, and Edward, on his marriage, lived at Rowling, near his wife's family at Goodnestone House, 11 kilometres (six and three-quarter miles) east of Canterbury on the Deal road. Jane Austen was a guest at all these houses, and would have been a visitor at others in their neighbourhood. Jane went to see Mrs. Knight at her new home in Canterbury, to which she moved after Edward took over Godmersham. Jane would obviously have visited the Cathedral and seen the town as well as making frequent shopping trips there. Mrs. Knight's house was called White Friars, built on the site of the old friary, but has not survived: shops stand there today. When Jane's sailor brother Francis was in Ramsgate, she most certainly would have visited him there.

Mrs. Austen's family, the Leighs, had branches at Adelstrop, in Gloucestershire, and Stoneleigh, in Warwickshire, and visits were made to both, as well as to her brother James

Leigh Perrot who had inherited from another relative and added their family name to his. By the time Jane was born the Leigh Perrots had sold their estates in Oxfordshire and had a house called Scarlets at Hare Hatch in Berkshire. Jane probably visited there as a girl, as well as staying with her aunt and uncle at the house in Bath where they passed the winter.

Jane's brother Henry had a succession of London homes at which she stayed as a guest: her friend Catherine Biggs married the rector of Streatham, south of London and her niece Anna lived in Hendon, further to the north, after her marriage to Ben Lefroy. There were also other friends and relations living near London in the vicinity of Streatham and Hendon. At Great Bookham, not far from Dorking was her godfather Samuel Cooke and his wife who was Mrs. Austen's cousin.

Closer to home was Ibthorpe, to which the Lloyd family moved after vacating the rectory at Deane, and then there were all those local friends in the neighbourhoods of Steventon and Chawton where they would sometimes stay overnight: Manydown, for instance, was much closer to Basingstoke and meant a much shorter drive before bed after attending a public ball.

Some of these places find their way into Jane Austen's books, either under their own names or as the inspiration for her own inventions. Over two centuries there has been a great deal of change in both town and countryside, but, although urban development in particular has drastically changed the appearance of places she knew and a good many of the houses she stayed in have long disappeared completely, a number still survive, little altered from her own day.

A huge increase in urbanization and the building of modern road networks have brought change throughout the land but much of the countryside and parkland offers much the same pleasure to the walker that Jane Austen experienced, though changes in agriculture and forestry may have altered the

The saloon at Stoneleigh Abbey, Warwickshire. Jane visited Stoneleigh with her mother and sister after it became the property of the Reverend Thomas Leigh, Mrs. Austen's cousin. This magnificent sandstone mansion, built around the cloister of a 12th-century abbey, gave Jane further experience of a grand house from which to draw material for her novels. The immense west building, with pilastered front and much other new work, was built in 1720. The interiors were, and are, of great magnificence.

In the 18th century, Lyme Regis became a holiday resort and it was a favourite place of Jane Austen, who visited it in November 1803.

Anne Elliott at Lyme Regis in *Persuasion*.

'They were come too late in the year for any amusement and, as there is nothing to admire in the buildings themselves, the remarkable situation of the town, the principal street almost hurrying into the water, the walk to the Cobb, skirting round the pleasant little bay, which in the season is animated with bathing machines and company, the Cobb itself, its old wonders and new improvements, with the very beautiful line of cliffs stretching out to the east of the town, are what a stranger's eye will seek; and a very strange stranger it must be, who does not see charms in the immediate environs of Lyme, to make him wish to know it better. The scenes of its neighbourhood, Charmouth, with its high grounds and extensive sweeps of country, and still more its sweet retired bay, backed by dark cliffs, where fragments of low rock among the sands make it the happiest spot for watching the flow of the tide, for sitting in unwearied contemplation; – the woody varieties of the village of Up Lyme, and, above all, Pinny, with its green chasms between romantic rocks, where the scattered forest trees and orchards of luxuriant growth declare that many a generation must have passed away since the first partial falling of the cliff prepared the ground for such a state, where a scene so wonderful and so lovely is exhibited, as may more than equal any of the resembling scenes of the far-famed Isle of Wight: these places must be visited, and visited again, to make the worth of Lyme understood.'

appearance of a particular view. But even in her own day, the work of Capability Brown and then Humphrey Repton, whose work as a landscape designer she mentions in *Mansfield Park,* were reshaping the countryside to create a new kind of English landscape.

With a little imagination the modern visitor may still be able to visualize a scene as it was in Jane Austen's time. What will be much more difficult to capture is the close familiarity and sense of place which she would have experienced. She would not have been able to make a spur-of-the-moment visit to the seaside or to Godmersham. It would have taken three days to reach Kent from Chawton or Steventon. A trip was a considerable undertaking and a visit would consequently be of some duration. This would have enabled Jane, not only to gain intimate knowledge of a town and its environs, but to make the acquaintance of many of her host's neighbours.

There were regular coach services across the length and breadth of the country but it was also possible to hire a private post-chaise should you be without a carriage of your own. Whether by stagecoach or post-chaise, a long journey would have required frequent changes of horses to allow the journey to continue with the minimum of interruption. The Royal Mail stagecoach service was very precisely timed. From Glasgow in Scotland south to London took two-and-a-half days. There were some scheduled stops to allow passengers half an hour for a meal and some others of 15 minutes duration where there was a great deal of post-office business to be undertaken: but in most places horses were waiting ready and a mere five minutes were allowed to get four horses changed and off again. Passengers would either have to sleep in the coach or book their travel

TOP
Lyme Regis from the Cobb. Lyme gained its royal title when Edward I used its harbour during his wars against France in the 13th century. Later the Cobb was erected to provide it with more shelter. Parliamentary forces were besieged here during the Civil War, bombarded from the sea by Royalist cannon. In 1685, the Duke of Monmouth landed here to lead the rebellion against James II. In the 18th century Lyme became a holiday resort and it was a favourite place with Jane Austen who first visited in November 1803.

BOTTOM LEFT
The Cobb at Lyme Regis, a massive stone wall curving out into the sea to protect ships in the harbour from the prevailing south-westerly winds and waves.

BOTTOM RIGHT
Granny's Teeth, the steps on the Cobb from which Louise Musgrove falls in *Persuasion.*
There was too much wind to make the high part of the new Cobb pleasant for the ladies, and they agreed to get down the steps to the lower, and all were contented to pass quietly and carefully down the steep flight, excepting Louisa; she must be jumped down them by Captain Wentworth. In all their walks, he had had to jump her from the stiles; the sensation was delightful to her. The hardness of the pavement to her feet, made him less willing upon the present occasion; he did it, however; she was safely down, and instantly, to shew her enjoyment, ran up the steps to be jumped down again. He advised her against it, thought the jar too great; but no, he reasoned and talked in vain; she smiled and said, 'I am determined I will': he put out his hands; she was too precipitate by half a second, she fell on the pavement of the Lower Cobb, and was taken up lifeless!'
Persuasion

Godmersham Park, the estate where Edward Austen was brought up after his adoption by his relation Thomas Knight. The property, which he later inherited, consists of rich parkland in the valley of the Stour, its watermeadows studded with enormous oak trees. Godmersham House provided Jane Austen with first-hand experience of living in the kind of mansion which she describes in *Mansfield Park* and *Pride and Prejudice* whose Pemberley is described in a very similar setting of rising ground above a river with woody hills behind. A handsome early 18th-century building designed as a central structure with two wings, it was altered over the years but the later additions were largely removed in a reconstruction of about 1835 which restored its original appearance as Jane Austen would have known it.

in stages. Private travellers would be able to make an overnight halt but would still need fresh horses at other stages. To travel with your own horses would mean proceeding at a much slower pace to allow them time to rest.

In *Sense and Sensibility* Willoughby, thinking that Marianne is dying and desperate to reach her, makes the journey of about 210 kilometres (130 miles) from London to Clevedon (near Bristol) in his chaise in only 12 hours, taking a ten-minute break at Marlborough to obtain some luncheon – but he must have had a change of horses. A more usual pace was just over eleven kilometres (seven miles) an hour with even less in hilly country.

There were a variety of different types of coaches and carriages in private use ranging from the four-wheeled

coach which could take six passengers to the chariot with accommodation for three passengers plus a box for driver and additional passenger. There were open, hooded and fully closed landaus, and light phaetons which often required only two horses. Two-wheeled vehicles included two-horse curricles and gigs, pulled by a single horse, which were the easiest to manage as well as the least expensive.

Mr. Austen kept a carriage at Steventon but this was given up when they moved to Bath but shortage of money meant that there was no question of his family having one after his death. But friends and relations would often send their carriages to pick Jane up when she was going to a ball and even send a carriage across country to collect the Austen ladies for a visit.

A view from Box Hill, Surrey, which Jane visited from Great Bookham and where she set a key scene in *Emma*.

BELOW
St. Lawrence's Church, Godmersham, beside the River Stour outside the walls of Godmersham Park, dates from 824 and has a Norman tower with its own eastern apse, once a chapel separate from the rest of the church.

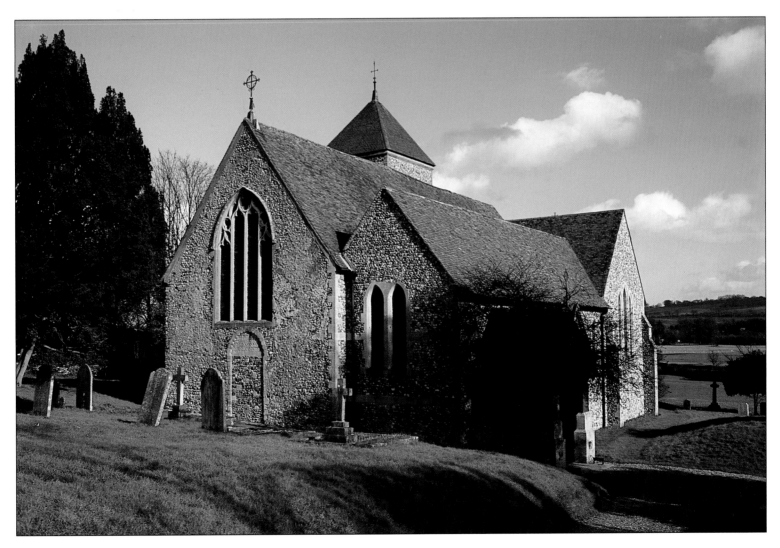

Canterbury Cathedral. Jane Austen would have known Canterbury well. Mrs. Knight's home, on the site of the White Friars priory, disappeared long ago and although Canterbury was heavily bombed in the Second World War, the magnificent cathedral and much of the old city survives. Indeed, bombing helped reveal some Roman features which Jane Austen could never have seen.

James's wife and children were travelling with Jane and since there was not room for all of them in one carriage James went ahead by public coach. It took eleven-and-a-half hours for them to drive down into Kent.

'At half after seven yesterday morning Henry saw us into our own carriage, and we drove away from the Bath Hotel; which, by-the-bye, had been found most uncomfortable quarters – very dirty, very noisy, and very ill-provided. James began his journey by the coach at five. Our first eight miles were hot; Deptford Hill brought to my mind our hot journey into Kent fourteen years ago; but after Blackheath we suffered nothing, and as the day advanced it grew quite cool. At Dartford, which we reached within the two hours and three-quarters, we went to the Bull, the same inn at which we breakfasted in that said journey, and on the present occasion had about the same bad butter.

'At half past ten we were again off,

and, travelling on without any adventure reached Sittingbourne by three. Daniel was watching for us at the door of the George, and I was acknowledged very kindly by Mr. and Mrs. Marshall, to the latter of whom I devoted my conversation, while Mary went out to buy some gloves. A few minutes, of course, did for Sittingbourne; and so off we drove, drove, drove, and by six o'clock were at Godmersham.

'Our two brothers were walking before the house as we approached, as natural as life. Fanny and Lizzy met us in the Hall with a great deal of pleasant joy; we went for a few minutes into the breakfast parlour, and then proceeded to our rooms. Mary has the Hall chamber. I am in the Yellow Room – very literally – for I am writing in it at this moment. It seems odd to me to have such a great place all to myself, and to be at Godmersham without you is also odd.'
Jane Austen writing to Cassandra, 15 June 1808.

Chilham Castle and the River Stour.
Chilham, a village of old houses clustered around a square with a 15th-century church, is only about three kilometres (two miles) from Godmersham. Chilham Park, where Jane Austen was the guest of James Wilman, an admirer of her niece Fanny, was once the owner of the property whose castle's 12th-century keep forms part of a Jacobean mansion surrounding an hexagonal courtyard.

WINCHESTER

Winchester is only 22 kilometres (14 miles) from Steventon and ten kilometres (just over six miles) from Chawton. It was close enough for James to have gone to Winchester Fair to buy a horse for Steventon and for Edward's sons to have gone to school there. Jane would almost certainly have made excursions from Chawton and would have been familiar with the remains of its Norman castle and its cathedral.

Winchester, county town of Hampshire, was the site of a settlement long before the time of Christ and was the Roman market town of Venta Belgarum. Here Saxons sought protection behind what remained of the Roman fortifications and as Witanceaster it became the capital of Alfred the Great's Wessex kingdom, and not only of Saxon kings but of the Danish Cnut and of William I after the Norman conquest. Here kings were crowned and buried and pilgrims came to the shrine of St. Swithin in the cathedral where he had been bishop in the ninth century. The great hall of the castle was where the Parliaments of England met for more than 400 years.

London eventually replaced Winchester as capital of the kingdom and the coming of the Reformation soon put an end to pilgrimage and swept away the monastic foundations. The ancient castle was largely destroyed in the Civil War and though Charles II began a new palace in 1683 it was unfinished when he died and was converted into barracks. Most of the old town walls were pulled down towards the end of the 18th century.

When Jane Austen moved into lodgings in Winchester in 1817 the town, after years of dependence upon the military and local agricultural trade, was beginning to assume a new character, making a bid to attract more commerce and visitors. Three old churches had recently been demolished to make way for redevelopment, there was a billiard room in Westgate and dances were being held in the ancient hospice of St. John on the north of the Broadway.

Jane saw little of this. On 24 May 1817, she travelled from Chawton in James's carriage with Cassandra and her brother Henry, her nephew William Knight accompanying them on horseback in the rain. She claimed not to find the journey very tiring, and 'had it been a fine day' thought 'she would have felt none', but was concerned about the men getting a soaking.

Their lodgings had been arranged by Elizabeth Heathcote, one of the Bigg sisters from Manydown, married and living in Winchester. They were at Mrs. David's, 8 College Street, behind the houses of the Cathedral Close furthest from the High Street. There was accommodation for herself, Cassandra and a nurse and they had a 'neat little drawing room with a bow-window' that overlooked the garden of the headmaster of Winchester College. Cassandra was not satisfied with the nurse and James's wife Mary came to take her place.

Doctor Lyford appears to have

8 College Street, Winchester,
where Jane and Cassandra lodged
and Jane Austen died.

diagnosed a 'wasting disease' which usually meant either cancer or tuberculosis, although there have been other suggestions that she was suffering from a form of Addinson's disease. Though Jane sometimes seemed to be in recovery and relatively free from pain, she may have been well aware that the prognosis was not hopeful. It was with a wry humour that she wrote to her nephew James Edward a few days after her arrival in College Street that 'Mr. Lyford says he will cure me, and if he fails I shall draw up a memorial and lay it before the Dean and Chapter.'

Mrs. Heathcote and her sister Alathea called at College Street every day and though Jane spent most of her time on a sofa, she was able to move from room to room watching the world go by from the windows. On another occasion she was able to take a outing about the town in a sedan chair and she looked forward to more and the use of a wheelchair when the weather was

Winchester Cathedral, the west front. The Cathedral of the Holy Trinity, St. Peter, St. Paul and St. Swithin lies in a hollow and it is only from the Close that its scale is visible from the exterior. A Saxon cathedral was rebuilt in 1079, the eastern part of which was reconstructed in 1202 and the nave and west front were remodelled in the 14th century. There were further embellishments and restorations in later years.

suitable. But her condition worsened. Her brother Charles came to see her on 19 June and feared that he was probably seeing her for the last time. Lyford had no hope and though he told James that 'he saw no signs of immediate dissolution but, with such a pulse – 120 – it was impossible for any person to last long.' Henry and James were now constant visitors and eventually felt it their duty to tell Jane of the seriousness of her decline. She managed to keep her composure and requested they celebrate

Holy Communion and administer the Sacrament to her while she was able to take it in full comprehension. Thus it was duly administered by them, for Henry as well as James were now both clergymen.

On 15 July, St. Swithin's Day, Jane appeared to rally and wrote, or perhaps dictated, a few light verses on the theme of the saint bringing rain to the forthcoming Winchester Race Meeting as punishment for holding them. They were the last thing she wrote. By

evening she was weaker, though she had slept longer in the night and more comfortably. Late in the afternoon of Thursday 17 July, Cassandra returned from an errand in the town, made at Jane's request, to find her sister recovering from an attack. She began to describe the incident in detail when she was again seized with pain. When Cassandra asked if there was anything she wanted Jane answered that she required nothing but death and asked that 'God give me patience. Pray for me, oh Pray for me'. Lyford was called and administered a drug to ease her pain, probably laudanum, and she drifted into unconsciousness. Cassandra sat with her, a pillow on her lap to support Jane's head. After six hours she allowed Mary to relieve her for a few hours before resuming her vigil. Jane died at 4.30 am on 18 July 1817.

The Dean of Winchester had given permission for her to be buried in the Cathedral and early on the following Thursday morning, so as not to conflict

The nave of Winchester Cathedral is the second longest in Europe, second only to that of St. Peter's in Rome. The overall length of the cathedral is 169.5 metres (556 ft).

with regular morning service, a small procession left College Street with the coffin attended by three brothers, Edward, Frank and Henry, together with James Edward in place of his father who was ill. It was usual for men only to attend the obsequies and Cassandra watched from the window. Jane was buried in the north aisle of the cathedral where a dark slab now marks her grave. A few days later, an obituary in *The Courier* made the first public identification of her by name as 'Authoress of *Emma, Mansfield Park,* *Pride and Prejudice* and *Sense and Sensibility*'. Henry Austen arranged for the publication of *Northanger Abbey* (his choice of title) and *Persuasion* at the end of 1817 (though they bear the date 1818). James Edward Austen, who had accompanied his aunt's coffin to its final resting place, published *A Memoir of Jane Austen* in 1870 with a second edition which included some of her early writings and part of the unfinishd *Sanditon*. In the intervening years, all her writings have appeared in print to the everlasting pleasure of her readers.

Jane Austen is buried beneath a dark stone slab in the north aisle of Winchester Cathedral. There is a brass memorial to her on the wall nearby and above it a stained glass window was placed to her memory in 1900.